Handbook for Christian Homemakers

Handbook for Christian Homemakers

Edith Flowers Kilgo

BAKER BOOK HOUSE

Grand Rapids, Michigan 49506

ISBN: 0-8010-5439-7
Copyright 1982 by
Edith Flowers Kilgo

PHOTOLITHOPRINTED BY CUSHING - MALLOY, INC.
ANN ARBOR, MICHIGAN, UNITED STATES OF AMERICA

Contents

In the Beginning

What Is Homemaking?

"We'd like to have you accompany us on our field trip," your son's teacher says sweetly.

"Could you bake three dozen cupcakes for the bake sale?" the Scout leader implores.

"Mom, I have to have a costume for the school play," your daughter informs you. "By the way, the play is tomorrow. Can you come?"

"Where's my lunch money?" your youngest queries three seconds after you start making pancakes.

"I can't find my gym shoes!" someone yells from the back yard.

"The boss is coming by the house this afternoon," your Prince Charming announces at breakfast. "Could you make a pie or something?"

"Would you help out by collecting for the humane society fund drive?" the friendly voice on the telephone asks.

"He followed me home," Junior explains as he forcibly drags a mud-covered pooch into the kitchen. "Can we keep him? I'll take care of him all by myself."

And the list goes on. You probably have your own familiar one-liners that you can add. Surely if any career requires wisdom (and stamina!), homemaking does. It's the most demanding, time-consuming, tiring, yet fulfilling and uplifting job any of us have to tackle.

Let's not confuse housework with homemaking. Housework is only one small aspect of homemaking. We all agree that housework can be, and often is, boring, tiring, and unrewarding. Why is it that no one notices when all the furniture is dusted but *everyone* notices it when we've skipped dusting in favor of a more demanding or rewarding chore? I've wondered why scientists haven't delved into this mystery instead of examining ancient burial customs of primitive tribes.

Homemaking is more than keeping the furniture dusted. It involves keeping a family fed, clothed, and on time for appointments. Homemaking *especially* means keeping a family happy. If a homemaker becomes more involved with the house than with the home, she has failed in her career.

Career? Is homemaking really a career? Isn't it just something all of us have to do whether or not we like it? Whether a woman chooses the traditional means of homemaking and stays at home full time or goes out to work eight hours a day and then comes back to her homemaking duties, homemaking is a career, just as is teaching or nursing or bookkeeping.

The Bible explains homemaking like this: "Every wise woman buildeth her house: but the foolish plucketh it down with her hands" (Prov. 14:1). Either a homemaker is wise and thus does what is best for her home or she is foolish and by her actions causes the downfall of her household. There doesn't seem to be any middle ground for indifference; the homemaker is either wise or foolish.

Wisdom, fortunately, is not the same as intelligence. Wisdom is an acquired attribute and it is available to any Christian who seeks it out: "If any of you lack wisdom, let him ask of God, that giveth to all men liberally, and upbraideth not; and it shall be given him" (James 1:5).

Who Is That Woman in the Mirror?

Are you satisfied with the way you are dealing with your homemaking career? Do you feel you are handling each chore that comes your way in the most efficient and most effective manner? Are you satisfied with the spiritual aspects of your homemaking?

If you answered yes to all of these questions, you are an unusual woman. I have talked to a great many homemakers, both full-time and two-career, who feel that they just aren't achieving all they would like to achieve. Some wish they were more talented and could sew or garden or make inexpensive customized gifts. Others wish they could make their houses look like the glamorous ones pictured in decorating magazines. Still others moan over their lack of patience with their children or their shyness in talking to their children about spiritual matters. Some complain, "I just can't seem to get organized." Do you find yourself in any of these groups?

I can offer no blanket solutions to the problems of homemaking. All of us are very much alike and, at the same time, very different. Some women love to cook and bake; others think take-out chicken is a gourmet treat. Some women keep an immaculate house; others struggle just to keep a walkway cleared through the middle of the rooms. Some women love fingerpainting with their toddlers; others love their children dearly but look forward to enjoying them more once they become adults.

Before you consider the ideas I offer in the following chapters for making homemaking easier think about yourself and your goals. What kind of homemaker are you? What kind of a person are you? What do you hope to achieve?

Take a look at yourself in the mirror. What do you see? If you are like most women, you will reply something like this: "My nose is sunburned" or "I'm starting to get crow's feet wrinkles around my eyes" or "I need to pluck my eyebrows."

3

If your answer is something like this, perhaps you can understand what I mean when I say that for most homemakers the biggest obstacles to effectiveness are lack of confidence, too much concern with outward appearances, and a tendency to look at negative points instead of positive ones.

Take another look in the mirror. This time try to see more of what is really *you*. Is your nose sunburned because you played golf with your husband instead of scrubbing the kitchen floor? Are those crow's feet wrinkles there because you laugh a lot? Do your eyebrows need plucking because you used your beauty time for telling a bedtime story to your child? The successful homemaker establishes her own priorities and ignores what "experts" say she ought to be.

Take a little time to get acquainted with yourself before setting out to revitalize your homemaking career. Realize that you are special to God and that He knows your talents, shortcomings, abilities, and assets. As He told Jeremiah, "Before I formed thee in the belly I knew thee . . ." (Jer. 1:5a).

Since God knows us that well, shouldn't we try to take time to know ourselves well enough to allow us to serve Him in the manner most effective for the person we were created to be?

What Do You Want?

When I was a bride I spent a great deal of time trying to make my home look like it was "supposed" to look. Since homemaking was new to me then, I looked around to see what everybody else was doing and then set out to do the same things. Early American furniture was featured in all the magazines, so that is the kind of furniture I had. Green plants were supposed to be growing throughout the house, so I struggled with some pathetic philodendrons. Everybody else had a dog, so we got one too.

The problem was I didn't like early American furniture or philodendrons. I didn't dislike dogs, but I would rather have had a cat. Eventually it dawned on me that what "everybody" was doing was not at all right for the Kilgo family. When I finally came to the point where I could run my household in accordance with my own tastes and judgments, I realized just how enjoyable homemaking can be. Living in accordance with other people's values and wants is a draining experience. It is rejuvenating to learn at last that no matter what some other homemaker is doing, it doesn't necessarily follow that the activity is right for you. Even worthwhile activities are not designed for everybody. Can you imagine the confusion if all twenty-nine mothers of the students in your daughter's class wanted to be such prime examples of motherhood that they all volunteered to be room mother? Or what if all homemakers got up one morning and decided to start making all the clothing for their families? What an impact that would have on the economy! Imagine what would happen if suddenly all the homemakers in the world decided to keep flawlessly clean houses regardless of the sacrifice. Who would tell the bedtime stories or sing in the choir or feed the bluebirds or create new ground beef recipes?

Be yourself. Only you can decide what is right for *you*. Just because your mother-in-law irons socks doesn't mean you have to. Learn what is right for you and your family and you've taken a big step toward creating a happy home. When the homemaker is happy it usually follows that the rest of the family is happy too, so when you accept yourself as you are and then know what *you*—not your neighbor or your sister-in-law or your pastor's wife—want, you have taken the first step in reorganizing your life.

Take time now to make a list of the things that you care about. Put the most important things at the top of the list and the least important things at the bottom. If home-cooked meals are more important to you than scouring the sink, you will know it when you look at that list. If having the house presentable for guests by nine o'clock in the morning is more important to you than is baking a batch of homemade bread, you will soon know that too. When you've finished making the list, you'll have a personal set of priorities as well as categories you can choose to ignore.

5

First Things First

I used to be surprised when someone said to me, "You're an organized person," or when someone asked, "How do you get so much done?" It seemed impossible that they could actually be talking about me. I never thought of myself in that way at all. Finally, one day after someone said that to me, I started thinking about my life and about how my attitude toward homemaking has progressed.

I haven't always been organized. In fact, I practically blush when I remember some of the messes I have made. There was a time when I couldn't seem to get anywhere on time. Also, I sometimes clothed my family by the "iron on demand" system—my husband got a freshly-ironed shirt one minute before he had to go out the door to work. Then there was the matter of meals. I like to cook and it pleases me to prepare an attractive and nutritious meal for my family. But when I first became a full-time homemaker I couldn't seem to get a meal ready on time. I would wait until an hour before dinner and then start deciding what I wanted to cook. The result was that dinner was always rushed, occasionally overdone or underdone, and less than a pleasure to prepare.

It wasn't that I didn't try. I tried so hard I thought I would fall over from exhaustion. It wasn't that I didn't care. I did care and I wanted desperately to be competent at the career I had chosen. It wasn't that I didn't know how to do the housekeeping chores. My mother worked from the time I was three years old, and I grew up doing housework and cooking. The problem was that I didn't have my life in order. I had priorities but they weren't the priorities I needed.

Have you ever heard the story about the man who prayed for an hour every morning? He said it was the only way he could get everything done. On days when he had twice as much work to do he prayed for two hours. That's one of the most amazing stories I ever heard! How could somebody do more after taking two full hours out of his day?

Most of us don't spend an hour a day in prayer and Bible study, but even if fifteen minutes a day is all we can manage, that fifteen minutes is the most important part of the day. The time spent in quiet communion with the Lord sets the tone for the entire day. Quiet time gives us the strength we need to be well organized or to do all the things we have to do. How do I know this? I learned it the hard way—which is the way that makes the most lasting impression. I can assure myself of a hectic, dissatisfying day by rationalizing that I'm too busy to have my quiet time.

I often complained that I couldn't seem to find time for an early morning quiet time. Most mothers can relate to this problem because our mornings are so full of filling the needs of our families that it seems impossible to find a few minutes to slip away for prayer and Bible reading. I kept making excuses until God at last carved out some time for me.

My husband's working hours were changed and we found ourselves getting up at half-past three in the morning so that he could be at work by five o'clock. Oh, how I suffered with that schedule! After Randal left each morning, I would try to go back to sleep, only to discover I was wide awake. Then by half-past six when my daughter was ready to start her day, I was desperately sleepy. That schedule was an agony! After a few weeks I decided to put that wide-awake time to better use: I used those early morning hours for prayer and Bible reading. Then the most amazing thing happened. After my quiet time was over, I could easily go back to sleep. When I got up again at half-past six, my day seemed to go much more smoothly. The difference was that I had learned to put first things first. After I had time to learn this important lesson, my husband's hours were changed again, and I no longer had to get up at half-past three in the morning.

The fact that it is necessary to prepare the heart before undertaking a task is underscored by Jesus Himself doing so. After Jesus' baptism, He went into the wilderness for forty days of prayer and fasting. The night before Jesus was crucified He spent time in prayer. If Jesus prayed for guidance before undertaking the things He had to do, can we as homemakers do any less?

The Bible doesn't specifically detail the household chores

a homemaker is to do. No matter how hard you look, you won't find any commandments relating to bedmaking or dusting. What you will find are guidelines for making those chores easier by learning to put first things first. Remember the story of Mary and Martha? To an outsider Martha might have appeared to be the more competent homemaker, but, since God sees the heart, He knew that Mary's motives were more acceptable than were the motives of her sister. Martha had not learned to put first things first, and, as a consequence, she allowed herself to become bogged down in chores while her sister enjoyed all the blessing. There are times when serving guests bologna sandwiches and inviting them into an undusted living room might be the better course of action.

Do you have more to do today than you can possibly do? Then why not start off the day with the Lord? Give Him your day and ask Him to bless it and to fill it with the events you need. This does not mean that God will miraculously make it possible for you to clean like a whirlwind and then feel like playing a round of golf in the afternoon. Rather, it means that you allow God to arrange your day in the way that He sees best and then cheerfully accept His decision. Sometimes "best" means that you won't get the refrigerator cleaned out or the windows washed as you had planned. Instead, you may be called on to counsel with a friend or to do some extra work at church.

I have found that when I yield my day to the Lord, it really doesn't matter if I finish the day with all my chores checked off the list. If I put first things first, everything else will be taken care of. Perhaps my mother will call and say, "I made about three times as much vegetable soup as we need. Would you like some for your supper too?" Another time a friend might stop by with a blouse her daughter has outgrown. "Do you think Karen could wear this?" she asks, thus sparing me the time-consuming task of going to the fabric store and cutting and sewing a blouse Karen needed for some special event. When I put the Lord's business first, He provides a way for my business to be taken care of too.

Do you want to be the best homemaker you can possibly be? Then "trust in the Lord with all thine heart; and lean not unto thine own understanding. In all thy ways acknowledge him, and he shall direct thy paths" (Prov. 3:5-6).

The Homemaker and Her Time

Lost: Golden Hours, Diamond Minutes

During my adolescent years my father frequently reminded me that "time and tide wait on no man."

The reason I heard this so often was because of my lack of concern for organizing time. If a book report was due in six weeks, I started to work on it the last day. If I had to be at a meeting at seven o'clock, I started getting ready at half-past six. If I needed a winter coat, I started shopping for it in March, only to discover that by that time the stores were full of summer clothing. Over and over I got myself into trouble because I didn't know how to manage my time.

By the time I married I was just about a hopeless case as far as organizing my time was concerned. But I still didn't realize the problem was *me*. After all, my parents had prodded me along for nineteen years, why shouldn't my husband take over the job?

It didn't work that way. Finally the time came when I

could no longer blame my problem on anyone else. The problem was me.

It is not easy to admit that dinner isn't ready on time because you didn't plan ahead. It is not enjoyable to realize a day has nothing to show for having come and gone because you didn't organize it from the beginning.

Time management is an important part of a Christian's testimony. A great many Christian homemakers who would not dream of gossiping or smoking or going about indecently dressed, sincerely believe they are doing their best for God, but in reality their lack of management within their own households subtly undermines their influence in the neighborhood and in the church family.

The Bible clearly states that time is a vital issue in our existence: "To every thing there is a season, and a time to every purpose under the heaven" (Eccles. 3:1). Yet time management is not something we know instinctively. It is learned behavior. In fact, it was so important that homemakers learn this worthwhile lesson that the apostle Paul wrote instructions that the older women were to teach this business of being "keepers at home" to the younger women (Titus 2:5).

Perhaps the ultimate picture of a well-organized woman is seen in the description of the virtuous woman in Proverbs 31:10-31. Here was a woman who cared well for her husband and children and at the same time managed to squeeze in all the duties she had to do. And those duties were considerable. They included spinning, weaving, shopping, feeding the household members, buying real estate, planting, doing charity work, preparing for the coming winter, sewing, finding time to look her best, running a home business, teaching, counseling, getting all the housework done, and producing children who admired and respected their mother.

Only a woman who managed her time effectively could possibly have done all these things. What then made her so successful? Proverbs 31:15 says that "she riseth also while it is yet night . . ." Did she plan for her "quiet time"? The verse continues with her first duties of the day: ". . . and giveth meat to her household . . ." The first task she undertook each morning was to see that her family had a nutritious breakfast. As the chapter continues, we see her engaging in all the other tasks she had to do. One theme runs throughout the entire passage: no matter what else the virtuous woman was engaged in, her effective time management allowed her to keep her husband and children as the real priorities in her homemaking career. As a reward for her diligence she had the one thing homemakers crave most of all: the love of her family: "Her children arise up, and call her blessed; her husband also, and he praiseth her" (Prov. 31:28). In spite of all the other things a homemaker might do, the ultimate test of success or failure in her career is found in her family. While it is admirable that the virtuous woman found time for all the activities that filled her life, all these things would have been mere "busy-work" if she had, through poor planning of her time, neglected her family's needs in order to do her good works.

What Is Time Management?

One time I read a book written by a famous circus performer. This man worked with the big cats—lions, tigers, and leopards. When he first began his career it was fashionable to call such a person a "lion tamer" but this man quickly discarded that title in favor of one he felt more appropriately descriptive. He was not a lion *tamer*, he insisted, but rather a lion *trainer*. Experience had shown him that the animals could never be completely conquered and tamed but rather that by the use of certain techniques he could prod them into conforming to his wishes.

Time management is a little bit like lion training. We talk of managing time, not taming it. No matter how well you plan, there will inevitably be occasions when things just don't go according to your schedule. Time management, then, is not total adherence at any cost to some preplanned list, but rather an ability to keep going in a competent manner when things go slightly awry. Just as that animal trainer had to think quickly and act immediately in order to stay in charge of the unexpected, so must the homemaker learn to react immediately and to replace inadequately functioning Plan A with alternate Plan B.

Time management is being in charge and getting the job done even when the alarm clock malfunctions and you oversleep by half an hour. It is being able to cope when the carefully planned meal you had counted on serving doesn't turn out because you forgot to plug in the slow cooker. It is peace in the midst of a storm not of your own making. Nearly all of us have experienced the electricity going off at the wrong time or the sewage backing up fifteen minutes before guests are due to arrive. These things do happen, and, while getting yourself organized won't insure that you will live the rest of your life free from such problems, it does mean that when these things occur you will have the serenity to deal with them.

How Is Time Managed?

One of the most frequently-quoted authorities on the subject of time management is Ted Engstrom, co-author of *Managing Your Time*. I would like to share with you my interpretation of some of the points he makes about effective time management.

Before setting about to remedy the problem Engstrom first puts it into the Christian perspective:

> Management of time thus becomes, for the Christian, management of His [God's] time. And this brings us to what may appear to be a slightly revolutionary thought. When times get out of joint . . . when tasks pile up . . . and when things go wrong . . . how often do we stop to ask God if we're doing what *He* wants us to do? It is *His* time we're managing, isn't *this* where we should begin?[1]

Having established the fact that God has promised to supply all our needs (Phil. 4:19), Engstrom then goes on to pro-

---

1. Ted W. Engstrom and R. Alec Mackenzie, *Managing Your Time* (Grand Rapids: Zondervan, 1967), p. 24.

pose that included within this promise must surely be the providing of all the time we need—as long as we keep ourselves in the center of God's will.

But how does the Christian homemaker, after having put her spiritual life in order, move on toward putting her homemaking responsibilities in order as well? This is done by implementing four effective tools of time management: purpose, goals, priorities, and planning.

Purpose is the starting point for your time management program. What is the reason you want to be more effective as a homemaker? It might include such things as wanting to be a better example to your children, wanting a more efficient way of doing necessary chores so as to have more time with your family, wanting to avoid the confusion and chaos which predominates in poorly managed homes, or even desiring to be a better Christian witness through your example of competence.

Goals are the second part of your program. It is not possible to manage your time effectively until you know what your personal goals for homemaking are. Your goals might be different from my goals, but that is not what is important. What is important is that *you* know what *you* want. Once you decide, it is just a matter of going after those goals. Let's look at examples of realistic housekeeping goals. Suppose you say that your goal is to have a house that looks as immaculate as those featured in the women's magazines. Is this realistic if you have young children and no paid household help? Could that goal be pared down to a more achievable size? Perhaps you will then say that you would like to keep your house as clean as your mother kept hers. That is more reasonable, but it still might not work. Was your mother a full-time homemaker, but do you hold down a career outside your home as well? Was your mother the kind of person who never went anywhere, but you busily participate in many outside activities? Let's try to pare that goal down. Could you be satisfied with keeping a house that is clean enough to be satisfactory to your family and tidy enough to prevent embarrassment when unexpected guests drop in? That is a more realistic and more achievable goal.

14

Priorities compose the third part of a successful time management program. If your goal is to keep a reasonably clean and tidy house, you will need to set certain priorities in order to achieve that goal. This means that you won't have to stop and wonder if you should make the beds and do the dishes first thing each morning or whether you should spend two hours reading a magazine. Because your goal is clear to you, the priorities in achieving that goal become clear also. A ringing telephone or a child's bruised knee may temporarily deter you from those priorities, but, no matter how many interruptions come into your day, those priorities are the things you keep going back to in order to achieve your goal.

Planning is the key to success in time management. No matter how lofty is your purpose, how beautiful are your goals, or how appropriately chosen are your priorities, the whole operation won't work unless you plan. Implementing a plan is easy compared to actually pulling it together for the first time. Planning involves sitting down and deciding how you will meet your goal of having the house presentable by nine o'clock in the morning. Will you make the bed as soon as you get up or will you cook breakfast and then make the bed while the breakfast dishes soak? Will you feed the dog and water the houseplants before tackling the things that show or will you take care of the more obvious tasks first? Your plan must be efficient for *you*. Your special circumstances have to be considered.

Success comes from putting your plan into operation. Have you ever gone into someone's house and received the impression that nothing ever got finished? Some dishes were washed, but others sat soaking in greasy water. The living room was vacuumed, but the cleaner was sitting in the dining room, thus indicating that the living room was the only room that had been vacuumed. The bed was made, but the pillows had not been put back in place. Yet, in all likelihood that homemaker had been working—the evidence shows that. Her problem, however, was not a lack of getting started but a failure to stick with each task until it was finished. You can work hard all day and be totally exhausted by bedtime and still not have a great deal to show for it if you fail to implement what Ted Engstrom and R. Alec Mackenzie call the $25,000 plan.

In *Managing Your Time*, Engstrom and Mackenzie relate a story which points up the value of staying with a task until it is finished. According to these authors, the president of Bethlehem Steel needed help with time management and went to talk to Ivy Lee, a management consultant. Lee's instructions were quite simple. He instructed his client to write down all the things he needed to do the next day and then to number them in order of their importance. Having established which things required attention first, these things were to be dealt with first. Number one had to be completely finished before number two was to be begun and so on. Lee suggested that his client try this method and then send him a check for what he thought the method was worth to him. Soon his mailbox contained a check in the amount of $25,000![2]

Fortunately we don't have to pay for the $25,000 plan, and the principles of it work just as well in a home as in a corporation.

Have you decided upon a purpose, chosen a goal, established priorities, and created a workable plan? Then finish it off by implementing the $25,000 plan and you are well on your way to an organized household.

2. Ibid., p. 53.

Creating a Workable Plan

What Does It Take?

Having once determined household priorities, how does the homemaker go about implementing the goals she has set for herself? It is certainly admirable to set goals, but it is even more admirable to achieve them, and no goal is achievable without careful planning.

Planning involves more than saying, "I want the beds made by eight o'clock, so I'll begin working on them at half-past seven." Planning involves not only the *when* but the *how-to* as well. It means having alternate plans available for those days when nothing seems to go right.

Careful planning also encompasses more than the mere accomplishment of a specific task. It also takes in our circumstances, temperament, and abilities. An idea that works splendidly for one homemaker might not work at all for another. For instance, let's take the goal of having the house presentable by nine o'clock in the morning. This is not such an overwhelmingly difficult goal, but let's look at the possible complications. What about the woman who is an "evening person" instead of a "morning person"? Some people function better later in the day while others leap out of bed with great vigor only to run out of steam by mid-afternoon. What about the woman whose husband works out-of-the-ordinary hours? It is difficult to achieve housekeeping goals when a husband is coming home from work just as the breakfast dishes are cleared away and he is getting ready to go to bed just as the children are getting ready to go to school. What about the woman who has two careers? It is a good feeling to leave home with everything tidy and clean, but, as any woman who has ever worked outside her home will know, some mornings it just isn't possible to leave everything sparkling.

The fact that complications not of her own making may interfere with her goals is one reason a homemaker can become discouraged and develop feelings of inferiority. All of us have experienced this discouragement at one time or another—it's almost an occupational hazard for the homemaker. It is difficult to resist comparing our achievements, or lack of them, with the achievements of other women, and when we do this we forget to take into account extenuating circumstances. When I catch myself comparing my achievements with that of another homemaker, I try to apply the brakes quickly. I examine the situation by asking myself a few questions:

Have I chosen a realistic goal for myself?   Sometimes it is easy to get caught up in what is "supposed to be" rather than in what works best for the individual.

Have I planned the best method for achieving my goal? Sometimes doing your best won't get a job done. If you don't believe this, try doing your mending by sewing with the blunt end of the needle. You can be sincere and work hard enough to exhaust yourself, but because the wrong method was used, your "best" didn't get the job done.

Have I matched the goal to be achieved to my temperament? At one time I wanted to add personalized decorating touches to my house, but since my budget was limited I didn't have the funds available to buy all the things that add that special touch. Consequently, I decided to learn to do ceramics. After only two lessons, I realized I hated making ceramics. It wasn't my idea of fun at all. Soon afterward, however, I learned to sew and discovered that creating decorative touches for my home was a delight. I had found the appropriate outlet to match my own abilities and temperament.

Have I taken into account the circumstances surrounding my goal? When I find myself wondering how another homemaker does this or that better than I do, I try to take into account the circumstances. Does she have children? Does she take an active part in church, school, and civic affairs? Does she have a second career?

In setting up your plan for achieving your homemaking goals, be realistic. Consider your abilities, temperament, schedule, outside activities, and commitments and then plan accordingly. Thus you will avoid the pitfall of having achieved a particular goal at the expense of making yourself and everyone around you miserable. It is possible to achieve virtually any homemaking goal you might set for yourself, but determine first if the results are worth it. Keeping a spotless house or being beautifully groomed or being the most active participant in church and civic affairs are all possibilities, but are they worth the cost? It shouldn't matter to you how wonderfully some other homemaker is achieving a certain goal. What counts is your own family and what is right for them.

Making Time

Do you know that you have all the time you need? All of us do. Even though twenty-four hours a day are all you have in which to work, that is enough time for whatever you want to do; you simply have to make time. Look at the other homemakers you know. Perhaps your friend Alicia delights in serving gourmet meals and your friend Diane excels at creating custom-made clothing and accessories. How do they have time for such time-consuming tasks? They apply the rule of priorities. If gourmet meals are important to you, that is what you will serve—even if the beds never get made. If you crave custom clothing, you will sew—even if the family eats TV dinners every night. The woman who knows what she wants to achieve usually achieves it—but it doesn't automatically follow that she achieves everything else at the same time. None of us can score 100 percent in every aspect of homemaking, and it is best to accept this fact and then proceed from there.

If you are a typical Christian homemaker, you don't want a lopsided kind of life in which one pursuit takes precedence over all others. You want a balanced homemaking career in which you do some of this and some of that. Consequently, you need more time. More time is acquired in various ways:

1. Eliminate the unnecessary. Have you ever been in the midst of some task and then suddenly stopped to wonder why you were doing that particular thing? Hard as it is to believe, a lot of homemakers spend a lot of time doing unnecessary chores. A workable plan ought to include the things that are important to you, but there is a difference between cleaning for the sake of cleanliness and cleaning because it is an obsession.

2. Forget about tradition, customs, and rituals when it comes to household chores. Who says we have to wash on Monday or iron on Tuesday? The best time to undertake any task is when it is convenient. Just because "we always give the house a spring cleaning in April," doesn't mean we have to continue the custom if it no longer fits our lifestyle. There was a time when spring cleaning was mandatory. After a winter of fireplace heating, woodstove cooking, and kerosene lighting, a house was coated with grit and grime, but that is not the way we do things today. Our houses are cleaner than our grandmothers' houses were after winter had ended. Why cling to a tradition that no longer fits our way of life? Likewise, for our grandmothers the "wash on Monday" idea made sense, but it isn't necessarily right for us. If you had to drag out heavy washpots, and boil huge quantities of water, and then scrub until your knuckles were raw, wouldn't you wash just once a week? But today a load of laundry washes while we cook dinner or read a book. Grandmother's custom just isn't right for us.

3. Don't measure your home by someone else's yardstick. I have a friend who struggled for years with the envy she felt because another woman was able to keep a cleaner house. Yet my friend failed to take into account one important difference: she had four preschoolers and the other woman was childless. It was only logical that the childless house would be somewhat cleaner and a great deal less cluttered. The amazing thing was that the childless woman envied the young mother too. She felt inferior and inadequate as a homemaker because she had been unable to have children. The result was two women were living the lives God had planned for them yet each felt inadequate because she measured herself by the other's situation.

4. Forget about "ought to." Why do so many homemakers feel guilty about their housekeeping? If two women go shopping, at least one of them is likely to say, "I ought to be home scrubbing my oven." Or at a women's fellowship meeting someone will confess, "I ought to be home cleaning my closets." In order to have a workable plan, it is necessary to eliminate "ought to." If a job is that important, assign it a high priority and then get it done. If it isn't that important, stop feeling guilty about it. It is easy to let "ought to" rule our lives, but by thinking about a particular job over and over we let it take up more time than it should. Most chores take less working time than worrying time. For example, one time I noticed a smudge on a window pane in my living room. Apparently someone had been looking out and had stuck his nose to the glass. My first thought was, "I ought to get some window cleaner and take care of that." Since I was on my way elsewhere, however, I didn't do the job. The next time I walked through the living room I again thought, "I ought to get some window cleaner and do something about that smudge." This went on for a week. Wasn't that silly? I put in at least an hour or two of worrying about "ought to" when the actual job of cleaning away the smudge was a thirty-second operation!

5. *Streamline.* Sometimes it is possible to add several hours of time to your week without sacrificing anything you really care about. How is this possible? The secret is to eliminate the timewasters that merely fill space. For instance, I used to watch the noon news report each day because I felt it was necessary to stay well informed. Then I discovered that by listening instead to the radio news report as I drove back from taking my daughter to school, I could save two and a half hours of time per week. Another timesaver was a new hairdo. At one time my hair was long, and I spent about eleven hours each week shampooing, setting, drying, and styling it. By getting a short blow-dry haircut I saved ten hours weekly.

Another way of streamlining is to look at the tasks you are doing and then try to figure out shortcuts. An example of this is found in the task of bedmaking. I once read an article in which the owner of a chain of motels described how his company saved thousands of dollars each year simply by instructing the housekeeping staff in the proper way of making beds. Most of us double our bedmaking time by running back and forth from one side of the bed to the other. The efficiency expert who studied the motel maids' techniques advised that they cut down on walking time by doing as much of the work as possible on one side of the bed before walking around to tuck in the linens on the other side.

In a similar manner, many other household tasks can be streamlined. Would a tray for removing dirty dishes from the dinner table mean you would save steps? Can you study the method you use for vacuuming and figure out a way to eliminate unnecessary movements? A savings of five minutes per day equals three and a half hours per year. Five minutes might not seem like much but three and a half hours is a big chunk of time and it is worthwhile to work toward saving it.

6. Enlist the aid of family members. Is there any logical reason why anybody over the age of four years can't make his own bed, pick up his own clutter, hang up his own clothing, and do a number of other household chores effectively? The idea of homemaking is to make a home, not to allow the homemaker to serve as maid for the rest of the family. Having the children participate in household chores is good for them as well as for you. It teaches them things they will need to know for setting up their own households and it also teaches them that the upkeep of the home is the responsibility of each family member that lives in it. Why should a ten year old care if he tracks mud into the kitchen if he has never had to mop it up and really has no idea of the work involved? Why should a teen-ager be careful with the car when he is never called upon to sweep out the debris and give the exterior a washing? Homemaking is managing a home. In most businesses, the manager is the person who makes the decisions about work and then delegates responsibilities. Are you *managing* a home or *running* a home?

7. Stop worrying about what "they" think. All of us have times when things aren't going according to schedule and we don't present quite the appearance we would like to project to the world. Therefore, when time is limited, it becomes a temptation to let the important things, such as spending time with the family, slip in favor of doing the more visible chores so "they" won't think poorly of us. Many mothers fall into bed each night exhausted from the pressure of keeping house for "them." But what "they" think is not nearly as important as is what you and your family think. If a child with an earache needs an hour of comforting, then the hour taken from cleaning house doesn't matter, regardless of how "they" might view things. I try to believe my friends accept me as I am—and it doesn't matter what the rest of the world thinks.

23

I also give my friends credit for having enough understanding and intelligence to know that, should they find my house in less than perfect order, it is because I had a higher priority that day.

When Things Go Wrong

The Workable Plan That Stops Working

Some days even a workable plan won't work.

No matter how well organized a homemaker is or how well she has managed her time, inevitably there will come times when outside problems will cause trouble. As long as the chicken pox virus exists and appliances can break down and husbands can be put to work on the night shift, homemakers are going to encounter problems in staying with a schedule. In fact, the most predictable thing about homemaking is its unpredictability.

The week I'm trying to get through now as I write this chapter is a good case in point. It's revival week at our church and we want to attend services every night. It's the time of the year when my husband is frequently asked to work twelve hours a day, and to work on Saturday too. The laundry situation is getting rather desperate because I've waited five days for the washing machine repairman. I have writing deadlines to meet and notes to study for a class I'm teaching. Added to this are two dental appointments and an unusually heavy load of homework for my seventh grader. Not only do I have twice as much as usual to do this week, but I have also lost my help to overtime work and to school assignments. Does this sound like a typically untypical week at your house?

Things are frequently off schedule in most homes. In fact, most of us couldn't define what we mean by a "normal" week. Because unexpected things do occur, we have only two choices: give up or cope. Since most of us don't like to give up, coping is our choice, but what a multitude of varieties lie within that choice! Do we cope by deleting things from our busy schedule or by staying up late at night to get everything done? Do we shortchange the family or do we take care of them first in spite of all the other demands on our time? Or do we do what we can in the best way we can and refuse to worry about the rest?

I have my own personalized "disaster plan" for such times. Before I work myself into a nervous tizzy, I stop and remind myself of a few things which are easily forgotten when things start piling up:

1. *This won't last forever.* It is hard to convince yourself that your troubles won't last forever when you have been awake three days and nights with a sick child or you have just been told that it will be at least a week before your car is out of the shop or you have just spent two days mopping water in the basement. Yet, hard as it is to believe at times, most things do get better.

2. *God cares.* It is hard to get past self-pity when things start to go wrong. Whenever I finally stop long enough to look at the situation in its proper perspective, I realize what I should have known all along: God loves me during the bad times as well as the good and He will give me the strength I need. Do I really think God cares whether I get the bathroom cleaned and the ironing done? Matthew 10:30 says, "But the very hairs of your head are all numbered." Since

God cares enough about me to even record such a thing as this, how can I not believe He cares about the things that distress me? Whether He is going to intervene in order that I might get my chores done is another question. What He *is* going to do is to give me that which I need, but sometimes what I need is not the same thing I asked Him to give me.

A recent incident with our washing machine points this out to me quite clearly. As all appliances eventually do, my washing machine stopped working. My husband tried to fix it, but, despite his best efforts, the machine would not work. Inevitably the laundry started to pile up, and I had no choice except to head for the laundromat on Monday morning. I felt so sorry for myself that I could understand how Elijah must have felt when he sat beneath the juniper tree. I beseeched the Lord to miraculously fix my washing machine. He didn't. I asked Him to fix my schedule in some way so that I wouldn't have to go to the laundromat on Monday morning—my busiest day of the week. He didn't. Off I trudged to the laundromat, discouraged, somewhat angry, and feeling totally unspiritual. Then, while I grumpily loaded three loads into washers, I noticed other women doing eight or ten loads of wash. While I inwardly groaned at being inconvenienced, they cheerfully accepted their lot. When I started to leave, one opened the door for me while another carried one of my baskets to the car. By the time I drove back home, I had learned the lesson God had for me to learn. Faced with the cheerfulness of those women in spite of the fact that they always have to wash at the laundromat, I felt ashamed. All I could do then was to ask God to forgive me for my selfishness and to thank Him for His care for me. Did He care about my laundry getting done? Yes, I believe He did, but He cared even more about me and my attitude, and that is why I had the privilege of being treated to a morning at the laundromat.

3. My family is the most important part of my homemaking. When you hit a bumpy spot and there are more demands on your time than you have the energy to meet, it helps to stop and reassess the situation. Is a clean house worth the loss of a night's sleep or being snappy with your husband and children? I would rather have my family enjoy being with me than to impress anyone else with my cleaning proficiency. This doesn't mean I will discard my mop immediately just because my daughter wants me to play a game with her. I will readily put aside household chores for important reasons or for a moment of fellowship, but throwing everything aside for a game and attempting to rationalize it as "mothering" is not helping the situation at all. Most of the time such a detour as this will only result in grouchiness later on. What child can feel "mothered" when, after an hour of togetherness, he has to face two hours of ill-temper? Balance is what I strive to achieve. I want a reasonably clean house and a family that is secure in my love for them even when I can't spend every minute with them.

4. Urgent matters need my attention first. During difficult times, such as when a family member is in the hospital, it is vital to separate household tasks into manageable categories. First come the necessities, such as food and laundry. Then come the things that need doing but can be put off temporarily, such as bedmaking, clearing away clutter, and dusting. Admittedly, these things shouldn't be ignored, but they aren't absolutely necessary. The third category is cleaning. Into this fit such things as vacuuming, scouring the sink, and polishing the furniture. These things are important but not as important as the first two categories. Last on the list are such things as washing the car, cleaning out a closet, or rearranging the furniture. These things can wait until the emergency is over. By categorizing duties in order of importance one can avoid getting caught up in a less important task while a more vital one goes lacking.

5. Everybody else hits bumpy spots. For many years I thought I was the only homemaker in the world who got bogged down in household chores. I believed that everyone else got everything done even when she had the flu or had unexpected guests or had three children with the mumps. We do hit rough spots and we do encounter times when it is not possible to have our homes look like the pages of a women's magazine. We feel we are the only ones going through such problems because we don't visit other homes when things aren't going well. It is entirely possible that the neatly dressed woman on the church pew in front of you on Sunday morning stayed up all night with a sick child and left her breakfast dishes soaking in the sink before coming to church. Outward appearances don't tell the whole story.

The Illusion of a Clean House

Have you ever tried to define what you mean when you say your house is clean? Does it mean it is freshly waxed, polished, scrubbed, vacuumed, and tidied? Or does it mean that everything is in order and apparent dirt or clutter is not showing?

At one time or another most of us have used both of these measuring sticks as a definition of *clean*. The problem is in the way we apply them. *My* house must be waxed, polished, scrubbed, vacuumed, and tidied in order to merit my approval as clean, but if I visit *your* house I see clean as the absence of anything to detract from the order of the house. I don't stop to find out if your house is waxed, polished, scrubbed, and so on. All I notice is that it is clutter-free and that the coffee table doesn't have a layer of dust on it. If it meets this test, I will probably think of it as clean, because I won't be peering beneath the bed to look for dust balls and I won't be opening cabinet doors to look for untidiness.

All of us tend to set higher standards for clean for ourselves than we do for others. While you won't think less of your friend for having newspapers lying on the sofa when you arrive for a visit, you would undoubtedly see yourself as slovenly if the same thing were to happen when she came to visit you.

A great deal of what visitors see as a clean house is merely an illusion. Without lifting a vacuum cleaner or a mop, a clever homemaker can, in an emergency situation, create the illusion of cleanliness just by putting things in order. Of course, it helps to be efficiently organized to start with so that in times of emergency "cleaning" can be done quickly. Here are a few of the things which can make a house appear clean even during emergencies or sicknesses when it is not possible to do a thorough job.

1. Get rid of the clutter. If all homes were run with the precision and efficiency advocated by home management experts, we would never encounter the problem of clutter, because all family members would put away everything without being told. But because all of us are tired or lazy at times, a certain amount of clutter will develop even in the most smoothly running home. Therefore, when time is short and everything seems to be going wrong, I start by getting rid of the clutter and, having won that battle, I am encouraged to work quickly at the next task. If time is really short, it may not be possible to put away the clutter. When my father was in the hospital I stayed day and night at his bedside and I went home only long enough to rest briefly, cook a meal, or wash some clothes. I couldn't take time to put everything in its proper place so I would walk quickly through the house and gather the misplaced items into a laundry basket and tuck it away out of sight. The house was not clean in the truest sense of the word, but with five minutes of effort I had the house presentable. A week later I retrieved and put away those misplaced items.

2. Do the obvious things first. Other than clutter, what are the two most obvious signs of lack of housekeeping? You probably answered "dirty dishes and unmade beds." No matter how clean the rest of the house might be, if these two things are left undone, the effect created will be one of untidiness. For that reason, these two things are high on my list of priorities even during times when my schedule is upset. When the clutter is gone, the dishes are clean, and the beds are made, visitors won't be nearly as aware of other housekeeping shortcomings. Then if after these chores are done you have additional minutes, concentrate on such things as cleaning the bathroom, taking out the garbage, and dusting at least the flat surfaces of the living room furniture. With these things done, you can skim by with the illusion of a clean house until your situation improves enough to make thorough cleaning possible.

3. Detract from housekeeping faults. Most teen-age girls are especially concerned with their looks and work hard at projecting the best possible image. Accordingly, one of the first things a girl learns is to dress in such a manner as to emphasize her good points and to downplay her bad ones. The same thing is true in housekeeping. It isn't possible to have all good points, so learn to emphasize what is good instead of emphasizing what isn't. If a friend telephones to say that she will be at your house in ten minutes, what can you do? Eliminating clutter and putting away the dishes will mean that you will have no time left to vacuum the living room rug. Yet you fear the rug will be immediately noticeable. The solution? Try detracting from the rug's appearance. The bowl of daisies you picked for the bedroom can be quickly transferred to the living room, and your guest most likely will look repeatedly at the blossoms and may not even remember the color of your rug much less that it needed to be vacuumed. Household conversation pieces also work well for this purpose.

4. Don't apologize. I have been in many, many homes while working with our church visitation committee and have had the opportunity to see many homemakers as hostesses. Although I deliberately try not to notice housekeeping flaws, some of these homemakers make it difficult for me. While I could move a stack of newspapers, sit down on the sofa, and forget the incident, most of them won't let me. Because of their embarrassment, they apologize for the mess and then make both themselves and me more aware of it by mentioning it. Offering excuses—or even good reasons—doesn't help either. I have been in homes that looked clean enough to me until the homemaker started pointing out cobwebs in the corner and dustballs under the couch. This is not part of hospitality and is not at all necessary. Most people who come to visit you do so because they are your friends and they really don't see as much of your house as you might think they do. (If you don't believe this, try describing the color and pattern of the sofa in the last home you visited.)

5. *Be at ease in your own home.* I can remember when the term "gracious hostess" was the absolute tops in complimentary phrases. What does it mean to be gracious? It doesn't have anything to do with how many rooms a homemaker has in her home or how clean those rooms are or how much the main dish cost or how many kinds of homemade chip dip are on the table. Rather, it describes a woman who not only can make others feel at home in her house, but makes herself feel at home there too. There is no quicker way I know—other than hiring a team of house cleaners—to make your house appear clean than to do the other things I have mentioned and then relax.

Being hospitable is somewhat easier than is being gracious. A homemaker who is hospitable makes her guests feel welcome—even if it kills her. A gracious homemaker makes her guests and herself feel relaxed. She is secure in knowing she has done her best—even if doing her best didn't include finishing all the chores she had set for herself.

How to Cope with "Hurry Flurry"

It is hard to deal with homemaking duties during times of stress caused by sickness, death, or imposing duties that demand our time. Yet, to a certain extent, we can accept the shifting of homemaking schedules because of real emergencies better than we can when the emergency is not quite so pressing. "After all," we reason, when we have committed ourselves to doing more activities than any three people could do effectively, "I said I'd do it, and I'm going to keep my word." Thus we set ourselves up for a nervous case of the "hurry flurries." While it is commendable to keep promises, keeping them can cause havoc on the home front.

32

The best way to deal with the nervousness that comes from hurrying to get everything done lies in planning ahead. If certain tasks keep cropping up, prepare for them in advance. Keep a batch of cupcakes frozen for emergencies or start on the new dress before the last minute.

But that doesn't eliminate the last minute flutters that come when you have done all you can do and things are still undone as a deadline nears. Here are some suggestions for getting all your tasks done.

1. Make lists. One of the biggest timewasters is forgetfulness. Therefore, the more I have to do, the more I depend on lists. It is distressing to make a frantic dash to the store on a day when you really don't have time, only to arrive home and discover that you have forgotten the main thing you intended to buy. It is tempting to say, "I can certainly remember to get bread, rice, and vanilla flavoring—only three things. I don't need to write it down." The result? Instead of spending three or four seconds writing it down, you will stand in the store for an extra five minutes, wearing a worried look and trying desperately to remember just what that third necessity was. You may even have to make a second trip to the store.

Lists also help organize errand running. If I have several places to go, I write down what I am to do at each place. Otherwise, I will get home with my stamps, only to discover that I have forgotten my postcards.

2. Eliminate the unnecessaries as quickly as possible. Sometimes results are more important than methods. Run down the list of "must dos" and determine which ones depend on the *what* rather than the *how*. Need cupcakes for a school party? A quick stop at the bakery will cost more but the time saved to be applied to that last-minute sewing project may be worth the expense. Eliminating the unnecessary step of making the baked goods yourself thus provides extra time for the other "have tos."

33

3. _Line up errands._ With gasoline becoming more and more expensive, most of us are becoming conscious of the need to drive less. Gasoline, however, is not the only thing that can be saved by lining up errands. Time spent in errand running is drastically trimmed too. For me this means scheduling shopping trips, banking business, grocery buying, and library visits either on my way to or from my daughter's school. Making each of these stops in a way that lets me go directly from one point to the next without backtracking saves time. It's a big waste of time to go out for one purpose, return home, then go out again for another errand.

4. _Recruit some assistance._ When I have taken on more work than I can handle, I have no qualms about asking for assistance—particularly of the person who has requested the extra task from me. If I already have an overloaded schedule and Karen wants a new dress made, I tell her that she can take on my chores while I sew for her.

Even preschoolers can help. Not only does having your child fetch this or that or answer the telephone make a few extra minutes for mommy, it also makes him feel important, and that alone is worth a few hours of compliant behavior. Children don't seem to see playing quietly in their rooms as a means of helping mother, but ask them to do a few tasks and it's a different story.

Getting Organized

How About Hide and Seek?

Do you like to play games? Most of us did at one time. I can remember that several of my childhood favorites were of the "hide and seek" variety. One person would conceal himself and the others would attempt to find his hiding place. On rainy days grade school teachers used a more limited form of this game. The teacher would hide a small object and the students were to guess where the hiding place was. Those games were fun then, but when you are running a household, "hide and seek" isn't nearly as much fun.

Were you ever rushing about getting ready to go to some important event, only to discover that you could not find the only belt that matched your dress? Have you ever spent an hour turning the house inside out in order to find a child's missing shoe? Or, most embarrassing of all, have you ever borrowed a book and then couldn't remember where you put it?

I have. At one time or another in my life I have managed to misplace practically everything that is possible to misplace. No matter how well I had planned to use my time, wasted minutes or even hours, were spent in looking for some object that couldn't be found because it wasn't in its proper place.

Maybe things aren't that way at your house. Perhaps your house is not only clean, but organized as well. It would probably take only a few seconds for you to name the location of some pertinent household items. For instance, do you at this very moment know where to find

thumbtacks?
insect repellent?
scissors?
the pictures you took on last summer's vacation?
the coupon to save one dollar off the purchase price
   of something?
a letter that needs to be answered?
the deed for your house?
the silver cake knife you got as a wedding present?
that wonderful handmade Mother's Day card you intended
   to keep?
the nail clippers?
the tweezers?
the burn ointment?
the card for your sister's birthday?
the spare pair of shoelaces you bought just in case?
the recipe you clipped out of a magazine last week?
the only love letter your husband ever wrote to you?
the transparent tape?
the pliers, hammer, and screwdrivers?

Did you score 100 percent? Neither did I! I was doing fine until I got to the spare pair of shoelaces, and that one stumped me completely! Even homemakers who have learned a great deal about managing the big blocks of their time frequently have problems in dealing with the little things.

Minutes constitute hours and minutes are what most of us

have difficulty organizing. It is possible for a homemaker to have her time schedule worked out beautifully with goals, priorities, and planning all adequately detailed yet face the little aggravations caused by things not being in their proper places.

A Place for Everything and Everything in Its Place?

Have you ever noticed how orderly are the things of God's creation? Everything God designed has its own place to be and, if not disturbed by mankind, God's handiwork remains organized and tidy. Polar bears don't try to live in Florida. The sun doesn't rise from the south instead of the east. Everything God has designed follows an orderly pattern and fulfills His purpose.

But it is not always that way in our homes. Sometimes it is difficult to find the things we want to find, and time is wasted in the search. Christians are expected to be good stewards of their time as well as their money.

Order in the Kitchen

Whether a homemaker loves to cook or whether she does it only because it is necessary, she spends a large portion of her lifetime in the kitchen. Several hours a day are spent in cooking, serving food, and cleaning up afterward. Yet this may not be the whole picture. If she cans or freezes vegetables or makes jams and jellies or homemade breads, the hours spent in the kitchen are multiplied. Plus she has to do all the related chores, such as mopping the floor, scouring the sink, cleaning out the refrigerator, and keeping the cabinets tidy. Some homemakers have their laundry facilities in the kitchen area as well, and this adds even more hours to the time spent in kitchen activities.

Is it any wonder that the kitchen is often the most disorganized room? Yet because it is a work space, it should be the most efficiently planned area in the house. I'm not talking about built-in appliances or time-saving small electric appliances. All those things are helpful and it is good to have them, but the real secret of success in efficient kitchen management lies not in spending great sums of money to update your kitchen, but in learning to make the best use of what you already have.

What is on your kitchen counter right now? Is it organized or cluttered? For many homemakers a cluttered kitchen counter is the biggest detriment to efficiency in the kitchen. Part of the problem lies with countertop appliances. It is helpful to have the things you use frequently placed in an easily accessible location, but how many of us use a mixer or a food processor or a blender every day? Why not put these things away and leave yourself more working space? For years I worked around such things and then one day I realized that a cleared work space saved more time than any other kitchen update. Consequently, for several years my kitchen counter has contained only two things: a canister set and a toaster. Such things as slow cookers, mixers, and electric frying pans can be kept elsewhere when they are not in use. The time I save in not having to work around these objects more than compensates for the effort spent in retrieving them from beneath the counter. Also, I save myself the effort of wiping splatters off them. Is there any homemaker who has not at least once lifted the mixing blade too soon and decorated the toaster, mixer, blender, can opener, and so on with drops of chocolate pudding?

Some homemakers like to use peg boards in the kitchen so that pots and pans or stirring spoons or kitchen aids can be stored neatly in one place. It is much easier to do your work when things are easily accessible and when similar items are stored together. The peg board idea helps to organize the kitchen and it might work well for you. Since I don't like things hung on the walls of my kitchen I prefer to store these items out of sight even though the principle involved is still the same: like utensils go together. My reason for not using peg boards or wall racks is that I like the uncluttered look and I hate to dust any more than I have to. When things are stored in closed cabinets they don't get dusty or develop a film of grease as they sometimes do when stored on walls.

Another problem is what to do with all those essentials that aren't groceries—such things as aluminum foil, light bulbs, cleaning supplies, laundry products, and paper plates. I pack two lunches every day, so I decided it would be worthwhile to designate a specific kitchen drawer for the storage of waxed paper, brown bags, aluminum foil, sandwich bags, transparent tape, freezer tape, and freezer paper. Since most of these things are on rolls, they fit neatly into a drawer, and it is faster for me to have all lunch packing supplies in the same spot. In addition I have added a small margarine cup with a slot cut into the lid. Into this cup goes the change which my daughter Karen takes to school in order to buy a cup of ice for her lunch time beverage. Also, a grease pencil is kept in the drawer for labeling lunch bags and freezer packages.

The same principle I use with lunch packing supplies applies to all other kinds of kitchen organizing. When things that are used together are kept in the same location, it eliminates the scurrying around that is inevitable when you are in a hurry and things aren't already coordinated. Keeping detergent, bleach, and fabric softener in the same location near the washing machine saves steps. Keeping paper plates, napkins, paper cups, and the picnic cloth all near the ice chest means I can put together a spur-of-the-minute picnic whenever the idea occurs to us. Likewise, in order to save time, keep cleaning supplies in the area where they are to be used. Oven cleaner belongs in the kitchen and bowl cleaner belongs in the bathroom. Decentralization of cleaning supplies saves many steps too. Buying several cans of cleansing powder saves time and encourages cleanups. Who is going to clean the bathtub after he uses it if he has to go all the way to the kitchen for the scouring powder? In similar fashion, who is going to scrub out the blueberry stain in the kitchen sink if she has to walk all the way to the bathroom for the cleaner?

No matter how spacious a kitchen might be or how many cabinets it contains, we somehow manage to fill them all up and then ponder what to do with the overflow. That is why drastic action is sometimes necessary in order to organize a kitchen. *Drastic* means getting rid of the unnecessaries. It is nice to have a few disposable pie tins, but isn't twenty-five of them a bit excessive? And just how many plastic margarine tubs does one home require? How about all those pitchers that outlasted the glasses that went with them? How about all those orphaned, one-of-a-kind glasses? Does anybody truly need two graters or three ice picks or four souffle dishes?

If this is the situation at your house, get organized by getting rid of the surplus. But wait! Don't throw it away! Try getting a few neighbors or friends together and swap your extras. Put your extras all out on a table where they can be easily seen, and let everyone choose what she needs. You will have a time of fellowship, a good feeling for having shared of your abundance, and, best of all, pleasure at having "shopped" for what you needed without spending a dime.

Order in the Bathroom

Sometimes I imagine what it would be like if five thousand years from now some archaeologist unearthed the remains of my house and found my bathroom cabinet just as I left it. I get a case of the giggles just visualizing it being solemnly unveiled in a display at the Smithsonian Institution. Can you imagine the erroneous ideas those archaeologists could get from examining the contents?

What should go into the bathroom? Despite the fact that bathroom cabinets started out being called medicine cabinets, I don't keep medicine there. Aspirin, vitamins, and prescription medicines seem more at home in the kitchen in the same cabinet where glasses are kept. Most medicines are taken at meal time, so why not put them where they are more easily accessible?

How about having cosmetics in the bathroom? That doesn't seem logical to me either. Since the whole family is often getting ready at the same time, why not put such things where they can be used without causing delay to some other family member?

Should first-aid supplies go in the bathroom? I don't think so. Often when someone gets hurt someone else is in the bathroom with the door locked. For this reason, I have moved my first-aid supplies to the hall closet, a central location.

What, then, should go in a bathroom? Since you have the nonessentials out, there should be adequate room for other things. Of course you will want cleaning supplies and extra rolls of toilet paper. If you don't have a closet in the bathroom, buy inexpensive storage units to hold towels and washcloths. This will eliminate the "I forgot to get a towel!" wail from behind the shower curtain. In deciding what does and does not go in the bathroom, I ask myself, "Is this item used *only* in this location?" Shaving cream, shampoo, bath soap, body powder, and toothpaste fit into this category. They belong in the bathroom, not in some outside closet. It is good to plan for emergencies too. Do you know where your plumber's helper is right now? The bathroom is a good place for it.

Order All Over the House

I'm glad I don't know how many hundreds of miles I walked before I learned about two of the keys to household organization: centralization and decentralization.

Centralization is putting related items together in one central location. You are probably already doing this to a certain extent without having to think about it much. You probably have all your shoes in one spot; all your stamps, bills, and envelopes together; and your umbrella, raincoat, and rain hat in the same closet. By having such things that are used in connection with each other located in one place in the house, you can save many steps and many minutes of time.

41

Are you tired of locating a pencil, then having to wander all over the house for a writing tablet, and finally getting your letter written, only to discover that you don't know where the envelopes or stamps are? If that is the case at your house, try centralizing a letter writing kit. You might want to invest a few dollars in a file box where not only letters to be answered can be kept, but where household papers and bills to be paid can also be filed.

Other naturals for disorganization include such things as cosmetics, sewing supplies, and gift wrapping supplies. Since all your cosmetics are usually put on at the same time, why not arrange them neatly on a tray or in a box used exclusively for that purpose? Sewing supplies belong together too. If you don't have a room just for sewing, it helps to at least have everything in one place so that you can pull it out and put it away quickly.

One of the biggest troublemakers for me as far as clutter is concerned is gift wrapping paraphernalia. Because I make it a habit to buy gift wrap and bows and cards the day after Christmas, Valentine's Day, and other holidays, I always have a good quantity of wrapping material to organize. So I grouped the materials according to holiday. There is no need to look through Christmas paper to find wrapping for a wedding gift. If less than a whole sheet of paper is used, I file it with the leftovers so that the next time a small piece of paper is needed I can go immediately there instead of wasting another new sheet. I also make it a practice to save boxes—preferably the kind that folds flat. It is usually possible to get a free gift box from clothing stores, but it pays to have extras on hand for other gifts. I also bought scissors and tape and pens for the gift wrapping box and that freed me from collecting these things from all over the house.

Decentralization is having related items in more than one central location. For instance, if you have a two-story house it makes sense to have both an upstairs place and a downstairs place for items such as light bulbs, furniture polish, and first-aid supplies. Even if your house is all on one level, it saves steps when you decentralize some things. When I realized how many times I was walking to the bathroom in order to get air freshener to spray in the family room, I bought another can for the family room. Sometimes things like scissors, tape, magazines, note pads, and hand cream are used in more than one place too. Putting a jar of cream in the bathroom and near the kitchen sink and in the family room means I can soothe my chapped hands in the winter months without having to trek all over the house to do it. Putting pencils in pencil cups and making them available in the bedroom, kitchen, and den means I am more likely to make note of things I want to remember rather than trusting them to memory. By keeping a pair of scissors in the kitchen, I bypass the problem of having someone borrow my good dressmaking scissors.

Shortcuts and Timesavers

Living by the List

For the organized homemaker, the one indispensable piece of paper in the house is the list by which she lives. Making lists of things to do or things to buy saves innumerable hours. It means you won't come home after spending your budgeted amount at the grocery store only to discover that you have no butter. It means you won't come back from a trip to the post office only to realize that you forgot to drop off your library books and therefore must make another trip. It also means you will be at home when the repairman arrives and you will be at the dentist's office on the right day and your friends will get birthday cards on time.

My list is more than just one sheet of paper. It is a purse-sized spiral notebook. In it I jot down the "to do" items and then rip out that page when everything on it is done. Likewise I note important addresses or phone numbers and then remove them after they have been transferred to the appro-

44

priate file at home. I also write down the supermarket bargains as the circulars arrive. Using this system, I can immediately discard the junk mail yet keep the pertinent price facts.

The other essential part of my list is my calendar. It has big blocks on it so that there is room to write appointments. Looking at my current calendar, I see such things as birthdays, the notation of the day when the appliance repairman is to come, the time of my appointment with the dentist, and a reminder to watch a television show on which one of my friends is scheduled to be a guest.

I also use my calendar for marking things I have mailed. Have you ever mailed off your income tax forms and, while eagerly awaiting your refund, wondered how long the forms had been in the mail? And if an insurance claim or a mail order doesn't arrive, I can pinpoint the exact mailing date by consulting my calendar.

Listmaking takes the pressure off when you are in a hurry because it relieves you of remembering things and lets you concentrate instead on doing things. For example, when I have guests over for a meal, I like to make a list of the dishes I will be serving. This lets me know in advance precisely what ingredients are needed and eliminates any last-minute dashes to the store. It also helps in another way. Did you ever prepare a lovely multi-course meal for guests and, after they had gone home, discovered you had forgotten to take the gelatin salad out of the refrigerator? I've done that. That's why I realize the value of making a list which can be put in plain sight. Mine goes on the refrigerator door until everything is finished.

For some homemakers list making involves the writing down of all household chores. I do this to a certain extent, but I see no need to make daily lists of such things as "cook breakfast, make the bed, scrub the bathroom," and so on. I already know those things have to be done every day, so why waste time writing them down? But I do make lists for out-of-the-ordinary tasks. No matter how well organized we try to be, there are certain little things that pop up unexpectedly and require our attention. I like to do these things immediately when they occur, but since that is not always possible, I make a list and then tend to the entire batch when I have the available time. My list of such items looks something like this:

> Copy down the recipe Martha asked me to give her.
> Sew the button on Randal's green shirt.
> Put the new snapshots in the album.
> File the cents-off coupons that came in the mail.
> Mail my aunt the quilt pattern she asked to borrow.
> Collect pine cones for my mother-in-law's craft project.
> Give away the magazines we have finished reading.
> Go through Karen's closet and take out the clothes she has outgrown.

What I enjoy most about coping with such a list all at one time is that when I have finished I feel so good about it. Each thing on the list is fairly insignificant when taken individually, but when I do them all at one time I feel I have accomplished quite a bit.

Another essential part of my list concerns clothing. I sew most of what my family wears and therefore I like to be prepared in case I run across some bargain-priced fabric. By flipping open my notebook, I can immediately determine the exact yardage required for a particular jacket or skirt.

Another use for the notebook involves the "want" list. Since some things are not essentials and don't have to be purchased immediately, I write these items down so that I can refer to the list when I am shopping. Even if it is three months until my father-in-law's birthday, writing down the blue sweater I hope to find for him means that I will remember to look for it in each clothing store I visit for other purposes.

The "want" list can include needs other than your own. For instance, I know that right now my mother is looking for a particular kind of wool fabric for making a skirt, and she knows that I am looking for a pair of gray shoes. When I go shopping it takes me only a few extra minutes to check the department store's fabric department, and when she goes shopping it takes her only a few minutes to stop at the window of the various shoe stores to determine if any gray shoes are available. Any time I am looking for some hard-to-find item, I tell several friends about it, and usually one of them will call and tell me she has located what I need. In return I do the same thing for my friends, and, consequently, all of us save a great deal of time and gasoline.

A Little Here and a Little There

One timesaver is to do a job five minutes at a time. You don't have time to clean the kitchen cabinets? Clean one shelf while you are on the telephone or while you are waiting for the kettle to boil. Five minutes' worth of cleaning several times a day ultimately results in clean kitchen cabinets without the mess and confusion of dragging everything out at one time.

A great many household tasks can be done on the piecemeal basis. For instance, why not clean the bathroom on the installment plan? Each person who takes a bath can scrub the tub. The bowl can be scoured just before you go to bed, and the sink can be cleaned in the morning after you brush your teeth. Taken individually, each of these tasks takes about five minutes, and it is easier to find three blocks of five minutes than it is to find one time block of fifteen minutes.

The little-bit-at-a-time cleaning system works well for jobs you hate to do too. Even if you do have a free two hours, the thought of cleaning a closet from top to bottom may be distasteful to you. But the thought of cleaning the top shelf or taking out the surplus hangers or repositioning the items on the closet floor doesn't sound so bad at all. Any of these chores can be done in a few minutes and is relatively painless when approached in this manner. Four or five times of cleaning parts of the closet result ultimately in a closet that is just as clean as it would have been if you had taken everything apart and spent two hours putting it back together again.

47

Hey, Wait a Minute!

If there is one thing homemakers are good at doing, it has to be waiting. Most of us would probably be appalled to know the total number of years—not hours, but years—we have spent in waiting. We sit in line at the bank's drive-in window. We sit in the doctor's waiting room. We sit in the car while the children have music lessons. No wonder so many of us are getting what used to be politely known as "secretarial spread"!

The resourceful homemaker can accomplish all sorts of things while waiting. Here are some creative ways to get things done while you wait:

Work on Christmas presents. Keep some pick-up work available so that you can cart it along to waiting sessions. Embroidery, macrame, knitting, crocheting, and other similar crafts are all portable.

Learn something. Have you been wanting to learn French or sign language or the rules of tennis? Why not spend your waiting time studying?

Take care of a small chore. While sitting in the car waiting for a music lesson to end, you can do all sorts of creative things. Try filing your nails or writing a letter or balancing your checkbook.

Use the time for prayer and Bible study. Most of us don't spend enough time in private study and meditation, and waiting can provide just the incentive we need.

Use the time for relaxation. It is good to use every minute in a constructive manner, but something is wrong when we come to the point where moments of relaxation are considered as wasted time. Jesus recognized the importance of relaxation and He told His disciples to "come ye apart and rest awhile." If a half hour or so of reading a good book or enjoying watching the leaves fall makes you feel good, then the time is not wasted. Sometimes the results achieved from a brief period of quietness and contemplation of God's goodness to us gives us just the recharge we need to cope with the rest of the activities of a hectic day.

Can Anybody Do Two Things at Once?

Have you ever seen a one-man band? It is a humorous sight. His hands play one instrument while his mouth blows on a strapped-on harmonica. His foot is hooked to an attachment that beats a drum. In spite of his odd appearance, the one-man band gets the job done.

Homemakers are sometimes a bit like the one-man band. It is rare for most of us to do just one thing at a time. We load laundry into the washer while the bacon cooks. We listen to a child recite his memory verse while our arms are elbow deep in dishwater. We pack lunches while waiting to add the fabric softener to the rinse cycle. Like the one-man band we look a little strange sometimes, but, in spite of how things look, we manage to get all of our work done.

One of the secrets of successful time management lies in being able to accomplish two homemaking tasks simultaneously. Can you imagine how long it would take to get everything finished if we put breakfast on to cook and then hovered over the stove without doing another thing until the meal was served and eaten? How about if we put the laundry in and then sat down beside the washer and read a magazine until the wash was finished? We would never get our work done that way!

You *can* do two things at once. Utilizing wasted minutes or even seconds makes it possible to do all the things you didn't have time to do before. While waiting for the bathtub to fill, you can rearrange the contents of the bathroom cabinet. While waiting for the tea kettle to boil, you can empty the garbage. Manicures, eyebrow grooming, skin creaming, and sewing repairs can be done while joining the family for an evening of television.

Talking on the telephone offers endless possibilities for doing two things at once. I can sort magazines, clean out my sewing basket, feed the cat, tie my daughter's sash, or even dust the bedroom while I talk.

Who says you can't do two things at the same time? You can and you do!

How to Have a Brighter Morning

We get out of bed and fall over something that shouldn't have been on the floor, but was there anyhow. Bleary-eyed, we stumble into the bathroom and discover that someone has left a wet bath towel on the floor. Next stop is the kitchen where late-night-snack dishes litter the countertop. All of us have a morning like this occasionally. Is this any way to get a day off to a cheerful start?

One of the best ways I have found to get more control of the mornings is by planning for them the night before. Prior to going to bed I make a quick tour through the house to see that everything has been put away and that nothing is left to put me in a bad mood first thing in the morning. Starting the morning with everything tidy is a good way to get a day on an even keel right from the beginning. It doesn't take long to straighten up the night before. Just see that clutter is cleared away and tabletops are left clear.

Another antidote for morning blahs is planning breakfast the night before. After I have cleared away the dinner dishes, I look in the cupboards and the refrigerator to determine what I will be cooking for breakfast. That way I don't even have to make any decisions when I first wake up.

For those who pack lunches, it helps to have that planned in advance too. Some types of sandwiches can be made the night before and put in the refrigerator. Snack food, such as raisins or nuts, can be put in the lunch boxes the night before. Such things as pineapple slices or cold applesauce can be put into insulated containers and left overnight in the refrigerator. If I am going to send along a hot dish, such as soup or stew, I set the insulated container out on the countertop so that it is in plain sight. Otherwise my homemade soup may remain in the refrigerator and my husband and daughter will come home wondering why there were only cold sandwiches in their lunch boxes.

I remember reading something in the newspaper when I was first married that made a great deal of difference in my getting things organized in the mornings. A young bride had written to ask an advice columnist why it was that even though she got up early and went right to work on her housekeeping chores, she never seemed to have things looking presentable before noon. I read this with great interest because I was having the same problem. The advice the columnist offered changed my housekeeping methods. The columnist suggested to the young woman that she establish priorities and, instead of zealously cleaning out closets or washing windows first thing in the morning, concentrate first on the more visible tasks. Her advice was to make the bed, clear the breakfast table, wash the dishes, pick up the clutter, carry out the garbage, dust the furniture, and then proceed to the heavier tasks. Then if an early morning unexpected guest did arrive, things would be in reasonably good condition. The problem was not that the young bride had not been working hard enough but rather that she had not yet learned which things needed doing first. Giving the house a reasonable amount of order first thing brightens up your morning and makes it easier to do the other tasks of the day. And if you are a two-career homemaker, coming home to a house that looks presentable is a good way to get your evening off to a good start too.

Is Anybody Hungry?

The Homemaker and Her Kitchen

Cooking gives women a greater opportunity to shape their family members' lives than any other area of homemaking. A gleaming bathroom won't see the family through the morning, but a nutritious breakfast will. A freshly-polished floor won't influence anybody's outlook on life, but the consumption of either sugar or protein will. A lovingly sewn slipcover won't change anybody's health, but well-planned meals can mean fewer visits to the doctor and dentist.

The power a homemaker holds when she takes charge of a kitchen is tremendous. Food preparation is much more than just filling empty stomachs. Proper food promotes physical, mental, and spiritual well being. Perhaps the most memorable example is found in the story of Daniel and his three friends. These young men chose to eat good wholesome food instead of the rich delicacies from the king's table. The result? "And at the end of ten days their countenances appeared fairer and fatter in flesh than all the children which did eat the portion of the king's meat" (Dan. 1:15).

Ironically, some Christians seem to have the idea that the body doesn't matter much at all. The body is only the "container" for the soul, they say. Paul, however, had a different opinion of the worth of the body. He said that the body of a Christian is a temple of the Holy Spirit (I Cor. 6:19), and that alone is reason enough to take good care of ourselves.

The business of taking good care of the body is not something outrageously impossible to do. Rather it is just what is *reasonable*. Paul, in Romans 12:1, says, "I beseech you therefore, brethren, by the mercies of God, that ye present your bodies a living sacrifice, holy, acceptable unto God, which is your reasonable service."

Back to School?

Would you apply for a typist's job without first learning to type? Would you be able to do an efficient job as a teacher without first getting an education? Of course, such ideas are ridiculous, but every day a similarly ridiculous thing is happening in many kitchens. Homemakers who don't know anything about nutrition are preparing meals for families and are inadvertently shaping lives—many times in directions in which they should not go.

Nutrition information comes about in different ways. We study the basic food groups for a day or two in a high school home economics course or we simply cook as our mothers did, and, if the food is nutritious, it is merely by accident. Some of us learn to cook by color. We like a meal to look appealing, so we add a colorful vegetable or a green salad. Yet none of this constitutes a real education in nutrition. Education usually comes about when a family member is diagnosed as being diabetic, hyperactive, or obese. It is a little frightening to get a crash course in nutrition in order to save somebody's life, yet every day some homemaker is having to rethink her menus because of the threat of high blood pressure or too much cholesterol.

The wise homemaker learns about good nutrition and then puts it into practice *before* sickness forces her to learn. And the learning really isn't all that difficult. The Government Printing Office has most of the information you will need in the *Handbook of Basic Food Values*. (Write to the Superintendent of Documents, Washington, D.C. 20402 for your copy.)

The Family at the Table

Does your family sit down together each day for at least two of their three meals? If so, your family is in the minority. Changing lifestyles mean that many families eat on the "grab and run" system. Dad grabs a styrofoam cup for his coffee, snatches two doughnuts out of the carton, and heads for the door with his "breakfast." Junior pulls out a box of sugar-coated munchies and makes his own "breakfast." His older sister takes a cup of black coffee to her room; she is watching her weight. Then finally everyone has been "fed" and mother can settle down with a second cup of coffee and a piece of pie left from last night's dinner.

It *does* take effort to get the entire family together for meals when you have conflicting schedules. But the effort to do so is totally justified by the results. In the first place, having everybody sit down together gets the day off to a quiet and controlled start. Then there's the matter of the food itself. When family members wander through the kitchen one at a time the cook doesn't feel guilty about letting them eat junk food, but if everybody is seated around the table, it is a rare mother who will place doughnuts, pie, sweet cereal, and coffee on the table and call it a meal. A sit-down meal encourages good eating habits.

Togetherness can also cut the grocery budget. Instead of serving food by the cafeteria method where everybody looks at what is available and then chooses his favorite, eating at the dining room table means less waste of food.

Going Shopping

Most women do the family grocery shopping. Even those who don't control any other part of the budget usually get a voice in the grocery spending. And most of the time that voice is a wail; it costs a fortune to eat well. But there are ways to cut a grocery budget. Here are just a few:

Learn to be a good steward. Sometimes it is easy to think of stewardship as merely giving God His portion of our money, but that is not the complete picture of stewardship. True stewardship involves all that you have, and your wise use of all your possessions, including your money, is part of your Christian testimony. Good grocery shopping habits are more than just a means of saving a few dollars. Your grocery cart is a silent witness to those in line behind you. The home-maker who honors her Lord with her grocery buying won't have as much difficulty with her budget. Once the whole process of shopping is committed to God, it becomes a challenge to try to constantly improve in order to present an even better example. When a task is done "unto the Lord" it is likely that the Christian won't hesitate to ask for the Lord's help. Have you ever gone into a store with only a little money and God stretched it for you so that you could buy the things you needed? Many times I have prayed for the Lord to direct me to the right store and the right brand so that I could buy what I needed at the price I could afford. Once grocery buying becomes a part of stewardship, it is not at all difficult to ask God to point you in the direction of some sale-priced potatoes if that is what you need. And does God honor such prayers? The Bible says, ". . . for your heavenly Father knoweth that ye have need of all these things. But seek ye first the kingdom of God, and his righteousness; and all these things shall be added unto you" (Matt. 6:32b-33).

Shop alone. Count on adding a minimum of five dollars to your grocery bill for each family member who accompanies you on a shopping trip. Even a toddler seems proficient at the task of making mommy buy more. Shopping with another homemaker is not a good idea either. If she buys something fancy or expensive you may want one too.

Make a budget and a list and stick to both of them. What does it take to feed your family for a week? Many homemakers don't know because they buy the bulk of their groceries at one time and then go back throughout the week several times for five or ten dollars worth of extras. Setting a price limit and then staying out of the stores after the limit is used up is a quick way to trim grocery costs. Another method of cutting costs is by making lists. Knowing precisely what you are looking for cuts down on impulse buying and shows you at a glance just how many more necessities you have to squeeze out of the budget before you can even start to contemplate buying an out-of-season melon for a special treat.

Read labels. Package designers are clever people. By making attractively-designed bottles or boxes they can create the illusion of more product than is actually being sold. Reading net weight figures is the only way to be sure.

Pricing is done cleverly too. Nothing is ever priced at a round figure such as ninety cents; it is always eighty-nine cents. By pricing it in this way, two things are accomplished. First, there is the psychological effect of making the potential buyer see the first digit and register the price as eighty cents rather than eighty-nine cents. Second, there is the likelihood of discouraging her from doing arithmetic to determine price per ounce since odd numbers are harder to compute.

Learn all the sneaky tricks. By learning to be as shrewd as the seller, the buyer can cut her costs considerably. Try buying fresh fruit and vegetables just before closing time. The prices are usually cut then. Ask the produce manager if blemished fruits or vegetables are available at a reduced price. Once fruit is in a pie, who is going to know you had to cut away a few imperfections?

Learn to look for bottles of bleach or juice or other liquids that are completely filled. Sometimes the automatic machines shortchange some of the bottles by an ounce or so.

56

If a price has recently gone up on a particular item, try checking the goods at the back of the shelf. Quite frequently a lazy stock boy has neglected changing all the prices. Since somebody is going to get a bargain in this manner, why shouldn't it be you?

Do your homework.   One of the intriguing things about the virtuous woman described in Proverbs 31 is that she did her own shopping in spite of having plenty of household help. Proverbs 31:14 says, "She is like the merchants' ships; she bringeth her food from afar." That sounds like comparison shopping to me! I just can't imagine anyone as thrifty and industrious as this woman was, not being a comparison shopper too. If she were living in our day, no doubt she would diligently study the grocery ads in the newspaper. She would clip all the usable coupons. She would know in advance just what she intended to buy and would walk into the supermarket prepared.

Learn to be creative.   One of the biggest bites in the grocery budget is in the area of convenience foods. At times convenience foods are worth the cost. During certain times of the year instant potatoes are cheaper than fresh ones and frozen orange juice is cheaper than fresh squeezed, but generally convenience foods are overpriced because the work is already done for you. What you are paying for is not food but kitchen help. A quick survey of some of the convenience foods you are buying may result in some big savings for your grocery budget. The price difference between flavored oatmeal and regular oatmeal is considerable. Likewise, the frozen vegetables with the special sauces or spices are much more expensive than the plain ones. Yet any reasonably competent cook can figure out that adding a sprinkle of cinnamon to her oatmeal and a dash of soy sauce to her Chinese vegetables takes only a minute and gives her the same result. Could a willingness to dash or sprinkle creatively cut your grocery costs?

Make substitutes.   When eggs are on sale it is cheaper to feed the cat a scrambled egg instead of a can of cat food. Pop-corn is an inexpensive snack that is more nutritious than sweet munchies. Ammonia is a cheap all-purpose cleaner that takes care of many household cleaning tasks and costs much less than specialty cleaners do. Powdered milk is fine for cooking or drinking once you get used to the flavor of it and it is much less expensive than whole milk. Investigate the warehouse stores where groceries are displayed in boxes. Try a few of the "no name" or generic products.

Learn the alternatives. A grocery store isn't the only place to buy groceries. Orchards and farms often have bargains if you are willing to pick your own produce. If there is a farmer's market in your locale it would be to your advantage to find it. Most cities have at least one outlet for day-old bakery goods, and this can mean a savings of fifty percent or more. Bulk grocers will sometimes sell to individuals too. It might mean that you will have to buy your mayonnaise by the case instead of by the jar, but the savings might be worthwhile. Try the co-op plan. Get a few friends together and divide a case of goods. That way all of you get the savings and nobody has a storage problem. Buying nonfood items at the supermarket may be costing you more than you would pay at a discount department or drug store. A discount store nearly always sells toothpaste, hand cream, film, hosiery, school supplies, and so on much cheaper than the supermarket does.

The Homemaker as Bodybuilder

What is in your kitchen cabinets, closets, and refrigerator right now? Are you feeding your family with sugar-laden foods or are you giving them what it takes to build muscles, bones, and intelligence?

Sometimes it isn't easy to feed your family in a healthful manner. With all the competition the health-conscious homemaker faces from television commercials, magazine ads, and other people's children, it is really a wonder any of us have had the courage to say no to all the enticements. Yet saying no is vital to a family's health, and the homemaker has the veto power to stop bad eating habits. If the concept of good eating is a new one at your house, here are a few ideas you might want to use to get started:

Decide who is in charge. Until I started discussing the matter with my friends, I thought most homemakers controlled their own kitchens, but apparently that is not true. "Junior has a temper tantrum if I don't buy his favorite cereal," one homemaker says. "My husband insists on plenty of colas and snack foods," another confesses as she wails over her ballooning grocery expenses. "I just don't feel right about serving a meal that doesn't include dessert," admits another whose size eighteen dress is a bit snug, "because it makes my family unhappy with the meal."

What is going on in all these kitchens? Obviously the homemaker isn't in charge, but why not? Since she is the one with the responsibility of providing for the health of the family, why shouldn't she do it in accordance with good nutritional principles instead of in accordance with family whims?

It is not easy to take charge of your kitchen after letting it be run as a family affair for a number of years, but it can be done. I know because I did it. At one time my grocery budget regularly included soft drinks, snack cakes, and other junk food, but once I realized the responsibility for my family's health was mine, I gained the motivation I needed to say no. There were a few wails of protest, but the dissension vanished within a week or so when it became apparent that I would not be swayed and that I would provide plenty of "goodies" that were not harmful.

Provide acceptable substitutes. The health-conscious cook encounters her first resistance when she tries to serve her family unfamiliar foods. It doesn't usually work. Soybeans *are* nutritious, but the family who is accustomed to meatloaf isn't going to look kindly on the cook who serves soybeans instead. Therefore, it is easier to retrain eating habits by beginning with alterations in the diet rather than by introducing

59

unfamiliar foods. Does your family eat too many salty snacks? Substitute raw almonds or raw sunflower seeds. Do they crave sweets? Substitute fresh or dried fruit. Do they like flavored drinks? Provide plenty of juices, both vegetable and fruit, to help them over the hump while you prepare to introduce them to plain water later on.

Learn to be sneaky with nutrition. I used to think I was being clever when I hid a few spoonfuls of bran flakes in my vegetable soup or cornbread or when I added a dollop of molasses to my baked bean recipe. But after reading Jane Kinderlehrer's book, *Confessions of a Sneaky Organic Cook* (Emmaus, Pennsylvania: Rodale, 1971), I discovered I was an amateur at being sneaky with good nutrition. Without her family ever noticing that she was up to all kinds of healthful antics, Jane managed to sneak all kinds of good food into them. Her meatloaf mixture contains healthful ground organ meats as well as the familiar hamburger, and no one is complaining. Her baked goods hide brewer's yeast and whole wheat flour, and her sweet snacks are made with honey instead of sugar.

It is possible to sneak a great deal of healthful food into your family without making them resent it. You must adapt your own favorite recipes in such a way that healthful ingredients are used instead of unhealthy ones. The secret is to keep the nutritious additive known only to yourself and to use it in a quantity that doesn't overwhelm the taste of the dish being prepared. You don't accomplish anything if your family catches on and refuses to eat some nutritious concoction just because "it tastes funny."

Eliminate the wrong things and substitute the right things. A large portion of the transfer to healthier foods can be made with no effort whatsoever. Fruits canned in their own juices will be just as well received as the ones canned in heavy syrup. The cook is the only one who will know if oils are used in place of solid shortenings. Natural peanut butter may be substituted for the hydrogenated kind without any problem—except that it tastes so much better you will have to buy more! Look for products that eliminate such things has BHA or BHT or sodium nitrite. Frequently, without giving up a food your family enjoys, you can simply change brands and thus avoid unwelcome additives. It is not possible to eliminate all chemicals from your diet, but with products where you have a choice, why not take advantage of it?

Make a gradual changeover. Now my family prefers brown rice instead of white, but I wouldn't have served it to them when I first began my nutritional program. Daily confrontations with unfamiliar foods is a quick way to alienate everybody. Instead, try adding one or two new things each week and never try more than one new thing at any particular meal. In that way, even if they do hate the taste of the new dish, they won't be in a bad mood because the remainder of the dishes on the table will be what they are accustomed to eating. I have gradually added such things as bulgor wheat to our breakfast table, lentils to the dinner table, and toasted unsalted soybeans to the snack bowl.

Make your own. It would be wonderful if all of us could grow our own vegetables, harvest the fresh produce at precisely the appropriate moment, and process it immediately before any of the nutrients slip away. That, however, is not possible for the majority of us. Instead, we have to learn to do the best we can within the framework of our own time, space, energy, and financial limitations. Made-from-scratch foods are undeniably best, but few of us have the time or the inclination for undertaking the preparation of all our food this way. How then, can the Christian homemaker cope?

My solution has been to decide which made-from-scratch dishes merit my attention and which ones do not. I would like to make everything from scratch but, since that isn't possible, I try to make wise choices. For example, I find the taste of canned green beans objectionable but the taste of canned tomatoes doesn't bother me at all. Therefore, I serve fresh green beans and then save time by using canned tomatoes.

Freshly-baked bread offers another choice. Homemade

bread is better tasting and more nutritious, but making it takes a great deal of time. I have to decide if it would be better to forgo homemade bread in favor of perhaps five or six other dishes which could be made from scratch in the same length of time.

Experiment with new ideas. Food preparation can be an adventure as well as a duty as long as the cook keeps an attitude of enthusiasm. Nothing perks up a boring routine as much as an interesting variation. For that reason I am constantly trying new foods and new recipes. With all the reasonably priced varieties of foods available at the supermarket, I see no reason to limit my family's meals to the same dozen or so menus repeated indefinitely. With this thought in mind I have been able to sneak a considerable number of good things into my family's diet without anyone noticing I was up to something. They thought I was just trying a new recipe!

Some foods that are loaded with nutritional value your family just won't eat. Liver and spinach are two foods which might be in this category. The key to getting such foods into the family diet is to stop pushing an unpopular dish and to experiment instead with other ways of preparing that particular food. For example, no one in my family liked spinach, and I thought it was a shame that such a worthwhile vegetable had to be excluded from our menu. Then I discovered that it wasn't actually spinach that we disliked; it was *cooked* spinach that we couldn't stand. Consequently, by serving raw spinach leaves in salad, I am still including a worthwhile food in our diet without making anyone unhappy.

Another good food is carob, which is usually described as a substitute for chocolate. Carob is good for you and makes delicious baked goods as long as you learn to enjoy it for its own flavor instead of insisting that it imitate the flavor of chocolate. It doesn't taste like chocolate, and I don't delude anybody by calling carob bars "brownies." They are *not* brownies but they taste delicious anyway.

Soybeans are another food that my family wouldn't eat. Then I discovered that if they are toasted in the oven, they make a crunchy snack that is a good substitute for salted nuts.

Get the Family Involved

It is difficult to change a family's eating habits after years of letting them eat as they please, but the results are worth the effort. In most instances, once a family starts getting the taste of real food, they will happily cooperate with the cook. The important thing is to go about changing lifetime habits in a consistent, loving, and sensible manner. Food is more than just something to eat. It represents a lot of other things to us—love, home, security, and pleasure. For that reason, the homemaker who suddenly pounces on all the treats and feeds them to the garbage can, substituting health food instead, is going to meet a lot of opposition. A four year old doesn't understand about vitamins. He just thinks mommy doesn't love him anymore if she stops buying his favorite junk cereal. Going slowly and helping him to understand is the best way to deal with the problem. Jane Kinderlehrer, author of *Confessions of a Sneaky Organic Cook*, advocates using a bit of psychology. A four year old who ordinarily wouldn't touch wheat germ loves it when the label on the jar is changed to read "Muscle Power," she says.

As soon as the children learn to read, get them accustomed to reading food labels. My daughter, who is eleven years old, has learned by now to read labels before asking for a special food. Since she knows that sugar is listed on the label in order of its percentage place in the food, she reads first and doesn't bother asking for that item if sugar is prominent in the recipe.

Mothers sometimes complain that the reason they can't provide nutritious meals is because the teen-agers in the family won't cooperate. It seems, however, that teen-agers are more nutrition conscious than many mothers suspect. Many of them are involved in sports and they hear their coaches discussing the benefits of good food. Others have learned on their own that some foods are harmful to the complexion.

Since the teen years are usually times of intense interest in looks, why not take advantage of this fact in menu planning? The same teen-ager who isn't interested in good food for the sake of his health, suddenly becomes much more cooperative when you start talking about pimples or muscle tone.

Husbands are usually the hardest ones to win over to more healthful eating—and usually they are the ones who need it the most. It is a challenge to entice a husband away from old habits, but the wife who is determined can do it—without nagging. It just depends on how hard she is willing to try. In my case, getting my husband off doughnuts-and-coffee breakfasts meant that I had to get out of bed at half-past four in the morning and prepare something nutritious. I don't function too well at that hour of the morning but, because I was determined, I staggered to the kitchen and gave it my best effort. Simultaneously breathing, keeping at least one eye open, and cooking constituted a major challenge to my early-morning will power. Soon I had him eating freshly-baked muffins made with whole wheat flour, wheat germ, bran, and honey. What stale doughnut could compete with that? Having once established the idea of breakfast, it was then a simple matter to move on to scrambled eggs, meat, and potatoes or grits.

Lunch was somewhat easier to deal with. Because my husband must take his lunch to work, it was a simple matter to substitute whole grain bread for white bread and to include a box of raisins and a banana. There is nothing especially radical in that. Then, as the weeks passed, I began slipping in such things as raw nuts or sunflower seeds or whole wheat crackers. All of this was done gradually and thus was almost unnoticeable. I also began talking more about food values— nothing incessant, just an occasional reference to plant the idea of good nutrition in his mind. I also shared with him some magazine articles about the particular benefits to be had from diet modifications. (The operative word here is "shared," not "pushed.")

I would like to think my family so thoroughly understands nutrition and is so committed to it that they would totally shun any kind of junk food, but I have to be realistic enough to know this is not the case. Therefore, I am not going to make myself and my family miserable by policing them constantly. I can control the food that comes into my house, but I am not going to embarrass them in public. I know Karen is going to eat ice cream, cake, and candy when she goes to a birthday party and I accept this and try to compensate by keeping her everyday diet as healthful as possible. Then when those special occasions do occur, we just accept them. Overzealousness can cause rebellion. A child who is never allowed the pleasure of eating cotton candy or an ice cream cone is missing a great deal of the pleasure of childhood— and he is going to blame mother. It is good to make your family healthy with what you feed them, but it is important to allow them a little freedom too. Children get a lot of pressure from friends and from advertising, and it takes a great deal of wisdom for a mother to know that saying no all the time won't work.

One Career or Two?

The Two-career Homemaker

How many careers do you have? Do you work at home as a full-time homemaker or do you go out to a separate career each morning and then return to your homemaking career each evening?

Increasingly American women are becoming two-career women. In 1980, for the first time in this country, the number of two-career homemakers (51 percent) exceeded the number of full-time homemakers (49 percent). This statistical breakdown, however, does not tell the full story. Included in the fifty-one percent are "empty nest" homemakers, single homemakers, and childless homemakers. Thus, the statistic in itself is not all that surprising. What is surprising is that forty-three percent of all mothers of children under the age of six work outside the home. This translates into seven million preschoolers to be cared for by nurseries, baby sitters, and relatives other than their mothers. As

66

children get older, the likelihood of their mothers going out to work increases. Among children of school age the number of working mothers is an astonishing sixty-five percent.

Today, more than at any other time in history, the question seems to be for many homemakers not "Shall I go out to work?" but rather, "How can I manage an outside job and my homemaking duties at the same time?"

The answer to that question is a complex one. Society encourages women to consider themselves free to choose a lifestyle but reality is a bit different. Women who work outside their homes are made to feel as though they must prove their capabilities superior in all areas. The result of this pressure to achieve has been labeled the "superwoman" syndrome. It means that the two-career woman is under a great deal of stress as she struggles to be all things simultaneously. Instead of cutting back on her home activities when she goes out to work, she may actually increase them. While most full-time homemakers can occasionally forgo some particular household task without feeling badly about it, many two-career homemakers seem unable to let anything go without suffering guilt.

How then can the two-career homemaker cope with the demands of both occupations without sacrificing the things which are important to her and to her family? Basically, it comes down to reacquainting yourself with yourself and at the same time learning to pare your ambitions down to realistic size.

How Much Time Does It Take?

Have you ever heard someone make a statement like this: "I can't understand why I can't get everything done. I work only forty hours a week. That still leaves me 128 hours a week for everything else."

The first problem is that the forty-hour work week is a myth. Most people live some distance from their place of employment, thus necessitating as much as an hour of driving per day just to transport themselves back and forth to work.

Many employees have an hour for lunch. When traveling time and lunch hours are added to that forty-hour week, it becomes fifty hours of being away from home.

Then there is shopping time. When you have to shop after work, when all the other two-career women are shopping, the chore is going to take longer. The lines at the bank are longest after four o'clock. The department stores are most crowded then. The result is a further erosion into that mythical 128 hours per week most two-career homemakers think they have available to them.

This, then, is where the solution to part of the problem of getting everything done begins. If you work outside your home, take a few minutes to calculate your own available hours for your homemaking career. Don't subtract just forty hours from your week, subtract travel time, shopping time, and, of course, sleeping time. (Why is it that homemakers always try to fit more things into a crowded schedule by skimping on their hours of rest?) When you have calculated your number of available hours, you will be able to assess more realistically what will and what will not fit into your homemaking schedule. But regardless of what time limit you devise as your starting point, please save yourself needless frustration by remembering one thing: no one, not even a two-career superwoman can do as many homemaking activities as a one-career homemaker, so why try to compete?

What Does It Take to Manage Two Careers?

Can you do two things at once? Most of us can if we have to, but it is difficult. In spite of the effortless look of the two-career woman portrayed on television and in magazine stories, real life isn't that simple. For the woman who works outside her home, getting everything done takes not only physical effort, but mental and emotional effort as well. Here are some of the components of successful career juggling:

Attitude.   Guilt is probably the most destructive item in the mental attitude of the two-career homemaker. She may have guilt over quickie meals, over a less-than-spotless house, and, most of all, guilt over whether or not the children are being adequately mothered. As a result, many two-career women tend to overcompensate. Driven by guilt, they lose sleep to clean house or to bake homemade bread.

For the woman who wants to be an achiever without being exhausted at the same time, guilt has to go. First, examine your motive for working outside your home. Is it because you must work to support yourself as a single mother or is it because you want to be able to buy extras for your family? Is your family happy about your job or are they constantly complaining about it? The decision to work or not to work is an individual one that has to be decided by each family according to circumstances. Whatever your decision might be, guilt should not be a part of it. Either improve your lifestyle so that you can dispense with the guilt or else give up the outside job.

Organization.   For the two-career homemaker organization is as essential as labor-saving devices are. You can't prepare quick meals after work if you have to make a special trip to the grocery store for some needed ingredient. You can't get the house straightened up in the morning before you leave for work if you have to spend a half hour looking for a missing shoe. Thus, if you are going to get as much accomplished as possible in the time you have available to you, get organized *first,* even if this means letting some of the cleaning chores go undone temporarily.

Cooperation.   Amazing facts: a child's personality is not warped forever just because he has to carry out the trash every day nor is a husband's masculinity undermined by his propelling of the vacuum cleaner through the house. While it is true that housework has traditionally been the domain of the wife, it is equally true that making a living has traditionally been the domain of the husband. If you are going to invade his territory, why shouldn't he be made welcome in yours? As the old proverb goes, "Many hands make light work." Isn't it better for everyone to pitch in and complete the chores so that everyone can enjoy some free time?

Streamline. Look at some of the tasks you do regularly and set a goal of trimming at least one minute off every one. If you could develop a streamlined method to take one minute off the task of making the bed, one minute off stacking the dirty dishes, and one minute off scrubbing the bathroom, you might find yourself with that extra ten minutes a day you need for some other task. Study your working methods and note any wasted motion. Then train yourself to eliminate that habit. If necessary, use a kitchen timer to encourage yourself to finish a task without dawdling.

Health. Only when you feel your best can you do your best, and this fact becomes readily discernible after a few weeks of shortchanging yourself on your sleep or your recreation or your diet. Whether you are a one-career or two-career homemaker, you need to keep yourself in top physical condition, but if you are a two-career homemaker, the failure to do so will become apparent much sooner. The human body is not designed to run well without a full night's sleep, invigorating exercise, proper nutrition, and the recharge gained from occasional periods of recreation and relaxation. Of course, if your schedule is already full, you may be saying, "But those things take time. I have a shortage of time now and I couldn't possibly fit in all those activities!" The body, however, is a demanding mechanism. You must find the time to take care of it now or you will have to find time later on to let it recuperate from the abuse it has endured. It's more sensible to maintain good health habits in the first place.

The Three Ds of Saving Time

For the two-career homemaker who never seems to have enough time to do all the things requiring her attention, I

70

recommend my system for coping with too much to do and too little time during which to do all of it. I call it the Three-D Plan because the elements involved in it all begin with the letter *D*.

Delete.   When a day has more demands than it has hours to do them in, you can systematically delete a portion of your chores. For example, suppose you have only one hour before leaving for work. There are beds to make, dishes to wash, garbage to empty, clutter to discard, and so on. All of these things *must* be done before you leave because you are expecting guests for the evening. But if you have only one hour in which to work, you are not going to get everything done. The result? Something is going to be left undone whether you want it that way or not. Consequently, it is better that you make the decision as to what to delete rather than to let a lack of time decide it for you. Mentally go over each chore and ask yourself, "What would be the result if this were left undone?" Then by analyzing the situation you can determine which chores have the highest priority. For example, if guests are coming and you can't get all your cleaning done, you can always close the bedroom door to hide an unmade bed, but there is little you can do to hide clutter in the living room. The solution? Take care of the visible areas first!

Delegate.   Although it is best when each family member has a specific routine of regular chores to do, sometimes you will need help beyond what is normally expected of the rest of the family. In times of pressure, why not let the rest of the family share in the hustle and bustle? I can see no reason why one family member, having finished his or her routine chores, should lounge in front of a television set while the homemaker struggles alone to finish some out-of-the-ordinary task. If company is expected or a special dinner must be prepared or the family is rushing about getting ready to leave for an outing, then it is just as much the responsibility of the rest of the family to help with the necessary tasks as it is for the homemaker to work on them.

71

Double up.   Doubling a favorite recipe can result in two meals for the same amount of work involved in preparing just one. Why not get two meals out of one pot of homemade soup or spaghetti sauce?

Doubling up works in other ways too. Using the same pattern, two garments can be cut out and ready to sew in the time it would have taken to cut out just one.

Doubling up on errands saves both time and money. While you are out buying shoes, stop for a loaf of bread, mail your letters, and drop off your library books.

Behind the Scenes

Are you equipped with the necessary timesavers to make being a two-career homemaker feasible? Many women are not. Obviously, if your entire paycheck is going to be spent each week on appliances and gadgets to cut working time, it is hardly worth being employed outside the home, but the purchase of a major time-saving appliance such as a dishwasher or microwave oven may be a good investment.

When you first start to work outside the home, acquire those things you need first, because once your paycheck starts being designated for this need or that, you will find it increasingly difficult to set aside the funds you need for labor-saving equipment.

It does help to have labor-saving appliances, and, if you intend to make full use of them, it is all right to buy them. But the kind of help which will benefit you most might not be such labor savers at all, but rather an acquiring of a larger quantity of necessary household items. For instance, the full-time homemaker who does laundry every day can get by with fewer towels, sheets, and undergarments. But when she goes out to work and changes her laundry time to once a week, more items are required. The same thing is true of groceries and toiletries. If she can set aside the needed funds to acquire a month's supply all at one time, she can save considerable shopping time.

Money, Money, Money

How Much Is Enough?

How much money would it take to make you happy? A million dollars? Or maybe just a thousand dollars? Enough to pay all your bills? Or does the amount of money you obtain have nothing at all to do with your happiness?

Sometimes it is difficult for Christians to get their feelings about money into focus. While we remind ourselves that "the love of money is the root of all evil" we also remind ourselves that somehow the rent must be paid. How then can the Christian homemaker learn to view money in its proper perspective?

Perhaps the easiest way to do this is to see money as merely one of life's tools. Of itself, money is neither good nor evil. What constitutes the good or evil in money is the use we make of it and the attitude that prompts that use.

As Christians we are expected to be good stewards of the money God has allowed us to have. The fact that attitude and not amount is the important thing is underscored in the Bible account of the poor widow's mite. While others cast in great sums of money they would never miss, this poor woman gave the most because she gave not from abundance but from love.

While Christians do need to understand the handling of money and to learn to be good stewards of their income, for some it is also necessary to guard against the opposite of greed—indifference to money. Have you ever known a Christian who went about blithely proclaiming that "my God shall supply" and then found himself in financial difficulties of his own making?

God *will* supply but He requires that we do our best with what He has supplied. Just as the wise steward in Luke 19:17 was commended for his intelligent use of the funds entrusted to his care, so we are blessed for our wise use of money.

Who Is in Charge Here?

Do you "handle" the money for your family or does your husband take charge of that responsibility? If your family is typical of most, quite likely you both have a hand in it. Yet some Christian women feel guilty about writing checks or making bank deposits. "Isn't the husband supposed to be in charge of the money?" they ask.

Larry Burkett, who has counseled thousands of financially-troubled couples, has some interesting things to say on the subject of money management. In his book, *What Husbands Wish Their Wives Knew About Money*, Burkett differentiates between the tasks of bookkeeping and the tasks of "handling" the money:

> It is important for both husbands and wives to recognize their joint responsibilities in the home . . . .
>
> The husband is the final authority in the home, but God also assigned some responsibility and authority to the wife. If the wife in the home can manage finances better than the husband, then she ought to be the bookkeeper. In fact, wives

are the bookkeepers in over ninety per cent of the homes. And there is nothing wrong with this.[1]

Burkett then goes on to say that it is the joint responsibility of a husband and wife to determine how the family's money is to be spent. Together they are to sit down and divide up the available funds so that all financial obligations can be met. Should severe financial problems develop, Burkett stresses that it is the husband's responsibility to deal with creditors. Because a woman's feelings are so intimately involved with her home, Burkett feels that a wife is the one who undergoes the most stress when her security is threatened and she is therefore ill equipped to deal with the pressures exerted by bill collectors.

Where Do We Begin?

A budget can put quite a bit of excitement into your life. Because of the budget, which is carefully planned and then implemented, you may find yourself suddenly able to do all sorts of glamorous things you were unable to afford in your pre-budget days. Isn't it worth a try?

Let's start with the Lord's portion. The word *tithe* means "tenth," and for many Christians this is the starting point for their giving. The tithe is scriptural. As far back as Abraham's time God's people were setting aside a tenth for Him (Gen. 14:20). In Malachi 3:10 we are told, "Bring ye all the tithes into the storehouse, that there may be meat in mine house, and prove me now herewith, saith the Lord of hosts, if I will not open you the windows of heaven, and pour you out a blessing, that there shall not be room enough to receive it."

After the Lord's portion of your income is taken care of, what then remains to be budgeted? The divisions will, of course, vary from family to family, but all of us have certain fixed expenses which occur month after month and must be taken into account when drawing up a budget. Write down

1. Larry Burkett, *What Husbands Wish Their Wives Knew About Money* (Wheaton, Illinois: Victor Books, 1977), pp. 84-85.

such things as rent or house payments, insurance, utility bills, car payments, charge account payments, and so on. Include grocery expenses, gas money, lunch money for the children, and any other regular expense which is part of your usual lifestyle. Next on the list comes such things as haircuts, school supplies, allowances for the children, and money for the coffee fund at work. These are the little items which eat up a significant portion of your budget without giving you much to show for it. However, it is a mistake to lump these things together under the heading of "miscellaneous" if they are regularly occurring expenses. "Miscellaneous" is the budget category that tends to get out of hand most easily.

Now tally these things up. If you come up with any money left over you are doing better than most American families are! If you don't have any left over, don't give up on the budget just because it looks impossible at first glance. We are going to discuss ways of getting things in line, but first it is necessary to see how much money you have available and into how many directions that money has to go.

You may have noticed that I didn't ask that you designate any funds for savings, emergencies, or even vacation or Christmas funds. These things *do* need to go into your budget, but first let's look at ways of getting the necessary expenses into line so that these savings funds can become a reality.

Trimming the Budget

If your outgo exceeds your income, it becomes immediately apparent that something will have to be done. Go back over the things you have listed and see if it is possible to trim any expenditures. Could you learn some do-it-yourself techniques to cut clothing costs, repair costs, or even haircutting costs? Could you pack brown-bag lunches instead of buying a noontime meal in a restaurant each day? Could you eliminate certain items that are there because of habit instead of need? Could you find creative ways of bringing in extra income?

Unfortunately for most families, when the budget won't

cooperate the first thing to be pared is the grocery allowance. I used to do this too. After all, it seems to be the most flexible part of the budget. It is not possible to do much about the house payment, but the grocery allowance seems to be a ready candidate for trimming. Being financially burdened, however, is hard enough without having to face the daily discouragement of beans and burgers for six straight months. My solution was to devise the lowest possible grocery budget which could still provide for nutrition and variety and then to learn to cook more creatively. By taking the grocery money out before paying anything else, I could assure myself of not having to face the panic of knowing it was five days until payday and I had only $2.65 to feed my family with!

Another way of trimming the budget is through the elimination of waste. Wise use of *all* our belongings is another means of stewardship. This means learning to turn out lights that aren't being used. It means lining up our errands so that we take the car out for one trip instead of half a dozen. It means cutting back on the heat and using the oven to bake more than one thing at a time.

Creativity in the kitchen can cut waste considerably. Do you find yourself throwing out a half cup of leftover vegetables or three egg yolks that weren't used when the whites were taken out for meringue? Learning to use every bit of food you have purchased can result in surprising savings.

Do-it-yourself is the best way to lower your expenses. Not only does it cost less when you do it yourself, but it may also provide you with some entertainment and some exercise. At our house we have tackled a little of everything, and, if you can read and are willing to pay attention to instructions, you can do the same thing. Fifteen years ago when Randal and I married, I didn't know anything about sewing, upholstery, refinishing furniture, gardening, or canning and preserving food, but I do now. Randal didn't know anything about repairing cars or fixing appliances or doing household maintenance, but he does now. All of these things were learned by reading library books, asking questions of our friends, consulting with the county home economist, watching experts work, and occasionally by making a big mess. Once we learned the wrong way to do something, learning to do it right was simple. If a woman who couldn't even lay out a pattern fifteen years ago can learn to sew well enough to run a dressmaking shop, and a man who didn't even change the oil in his car fifteen years ago can learn to do major car repairs, then there is hope for anybody in the do-it-yourself field.

Another creative way of cutting costs is through sharing and bartering. If your garden yields more tomatoes than you can use, why not ask your neighbor if she would like a bushel of tomatoes in exchange for a piece of her handmade jewelry? Without spending a cent you have made her happy and have acquired a gift which can be put away for future occasions. Services, too, can be swapped. Because people have different likes and dislikes, it's possible you can work out a deal to save yourself both money and exasperation. If you like to paint but hate to rake leaves, it's likely you can find a friend who loves raking leaves but hates painting.

Another possibility is sharing. My husband and my father seem to be engaged in a continuous round robin of exchange. One of them—and for me it's hard to tell which one—owns a post-hole digger and a stepladder. The other one owns an extension ladder and a garden tiller. By sharing, both of them cut down on expense and storage.

The most effective budget trimmer of all is what I call "plugging up the leaks." Or as my father says, "Watch out for your pennies and your dollars will watch out for themselves." Have you ever noticed how many quarters and dimes and nickels it takes to put a child through school? Or how many pennies it takes to pay deposits on bottles that never get taken back to the grocery store? Or how many unnecessary gadgets come into the home simply because they cost "only" fifty-nine cents? These are some of the leaks that cause havoc with any budget.

Before buying anything that is not designated in your budget, try asking yourself these questions: Do I need this item? Why do I want it? Will the use received from it justify the expense? What do I already have on hand that could be substituted for this item in order to avoid the expenditure?

78

Another frequent source of leaks in the budget is the money parceled out to children. The younger members of the family deserve a portion of the family income and, like the adults, enjoy snacks and entertainment. This, however, is one area where a great deal of money can be dribbled away from the budget unless parents are careful. The best course of action may be a fixed allowance. When a child has his own money and is taught to live within his means right from his toddler days, it is not nearly as likely that he will grow up to be irresponsible in handling his funds. The amount a child receives depends on many factors. Will he be using the money simply for pleasure or will he also have certain "bills" to handle as well? It helps to inspire bargain-hunting habits in young ones if they are allowed to handle part of their own expenses.

Perhaps the biggest trouble spot in most budgets is the overspending for favorite activities or special interest items. This might include such things as bowling or tennis or jewelry or even special foods. All of us seem to have at least one area in which we are more easily tempted than in others. For me it is fabric. Of course, if your pet temptation is a thing such as clothing, fabric, or food, that makes it all the harder to deal with. We rationalize these things and convince ourselves that we are not overspending but are just stocking up. The only way to deal with such a situation is to set a specific dollar limit and then force yourself to stick with the limits. This means avoiding going to the store when you don't have the money for impulse spending on your favorite frivolity. It also means leaving credit cards and checkbooks at home when you go into such places so that you are not tempted to spend beyond that which you have budgeted.

Another effective way to avoid overspending is by designating a small amount of money for personal use. This is an allotment which both husband and wife have and which can be spent precisely as either one chooses without an explanation or a rationalization. The amount doesn't have to be large, in fact, it almost seems as though the smaller the amount is the more enjoyable it becomes. It is like the days in your childhood when you had only one dime to spend and the candy counter beckoned with so many alluring choices. Even a sum as small as five dollars a week for "throwaway" money can make you feel much better about your budget. Ironically, just knowing the "throwaway" money is in your wallet may curb your spending because it serves to relieve you of that deprived feeling we all tend to get when our budgets are tight and we never have the joy of buying anything just for the fun of it. The result? You will be surprised at how few times you will actually waste that throwaway money.

The Christian and Credit

Is it permissible for Christians to use credit? This question puzzles many. With today's economy being what it is, few of us could ever own a house or an automobile without the aid of credit. But the real problem with credit doesn't seem to be in its use for such things as houses and cars but in its use for day-to-day living expenses.

Money problems are one of the major causes of divorce. That fact alone should be enough to scare most of us away from unwise use of credit. But with credit so easy to obtain and so socially acceptable, it is easy for families to get in over their heads financially.

Women, in particular, seem especially vulnerable to credit card problems. Perhaps one of the major reasons for this is that the homemaker does most of the family's shopping. Being frequently exposed to the temptation to "buy now, pay later" tends to break down resistance. Women have traditionally been the ones to make their houses into havens for the rest of their family, and, because we like to create a feeling of comfort and security, it becomes difficult for many of us to restrain ourselves from overspending.

What then can be done for the family who has already overburdened itself through the unwise use of credit? There is only one way out: destroy or lock away credit cards until the situation can be improved. You can't get out of debt by continuing to use credit. Then after dealing with the debts, perhaps you will discover that you don't ever want to go back to credit cards again. Many Christians do successfully get by without using any credit cards at all and spend less because of it. There is a restraint factor built into the act of pulling cash money out of your purse in order to buy an item you want.

How can a family determine if they are getting too deeply involved in the use of credit? Money management specialists suggest the use of several questions to use as a guideline: Are you using the credit cards to cover the cost of day-to-day expenses such as food or gasoline? Are you finding it a more frequent occurrence that the incoming bills must be juggled because you are not able to pay installments on all of them at the same time? Do you currently owe more than you could pay off if all your assets were liquidated? Are you creating charge bills at a faster rate than you are paying them off? Have you totally given up savings because you have nothing left to deposit into savings after all the bills are paid? "Yes" answers to one or more of these questions indicates a dangerous involvement in credit buying.

A Penny Saved Is a Penny Earned—Sometimes

Have you ever watched a squirrel busily carrying nuts to be stashed away for the coming winter? Somehow he knows that in order to survive the hard times ahead of him, he must make adequate provisions. When the hard days of winter arrive he is secure in knowing that his "savings account" will tide him over until things improve.

God has built this instinct into many of His creatures. Yet somehow human beings don't seem too inclined to heed the call to preparation for the future. Some even think it sinful to save money. They see it as a failure to rely on God's ability to supply on a day-to-day basis. While the Bible does warn against the love of money—and hoarding money does constitute love of it—the Bible does not condemn prudence. We are told, "Go to the ant, thou sluggard; consider her ways, and be wise: Which having no guide, overseer, or ruler, provideth her meat in the summer, and gathereth her food in the harvest" (Prov. 6:6-8).

God will supply all our needs, even on a day-to-day basis if that is what our lifestyle requires. Yet at times when He is supplying more than is needed for each day, does it seem logical that He would want us to squander it foolishly just so we might go to Him the next day with an empty hand to receive more? That wasn't God's plan during the years when He was blessing the land of Egypt with plenty in order that the people might prepare for the years of famine (Gen. 41:28-36).

For the Christian who seeks to be a good steward and to put aside money for the possible lean times ahead, there are a multitude of choices. While Pharaoh had only to store his "savings" in barns, we have to choose between savings accounts, credit union accounts, savings bonds, Christmas club accounts, certificates of deposit, and so on.

First, there is the puzzle of how much to save. A figure that is frequently mentioned by the experts is 10 percent. Since this is a sizable chunk of the family income, many families have found that the only way to put aside such a sum is through payroll deductions or through automatic withdrawals from their checking account. The idea is that you can't miss money you never got your hands on in the first place.

With double-digit inflation continuing to plague this country, old ideas about savings have had to be rethought. While passbook savings accounts were once considered the safest and wisest means of saving, now they are only considered safe. If you opened up a savings account of one thousand dollars today and then received interest on it all year, at the end of the year your savings account plus the interest it had accumulated would actually buy less than the original one thousand dollars would have bought a year earlier. In effect, inflation would have penalized you for your thriftiness.

For this reason, such accounts should be used only for specific short-term purposes, such as a means of acquiring a few hundred dollars for a special project, as a way to accumulate enough cash to buy a certificate of deposit, which will pay you more than double the interest you can get from a savings account, or as a resting place for a few hundred dollars you might want to keep available as a means of acquiring quick cash for an unexpected expense.

Christmas club accounts usually pay even less interest than a regular passbook savings account and this means that you will lose even more in the battle with inflation.

Checking accounts that pay interest have a catch to them too. Some banks require that you maintain a minimum daily balance as high as one thousand dollars, and this means that you are tying up that much money in a low-interest account rather than in a certificate of deposit which would show more profit.

Government savings bonds are probably the least attractive means of saving available right now. It is handy to have them taken out as a payroll deduction before you get a chance to spend the money elsewhere, but the convenience is offset by an interest rate that is not competitive with more attractive investments in savings that you can make elsewhere.

Can I Make Money at Home?

Today's Choices

One of the nicest things about being a twentieth-century homemaker is that we can choose our career. No longer are women rushed into marriage and childbearing because that is "the way it is supposed to be." Those of us who are one-career homemakers have had the privilege of choosing this role. As a result, forty-nine percent of the women in this country do not work at an additional job outside their homes.

Our problem lies not in the choosing but in today's precarious economic situation. We are all victims of double-digit inflation, which makes it increasingly difficult to make income keep pace with prices. The result of such a dilemma is a predictable one. The family income is not enough? Put mama to work! Consequently, in many homes mama has gone out to work although she really didn't prefer to do so.

When things get desperate financially, some families consider another alternative to having the full-time homemaker go out to work: the husband gets a second job. But the results of this solution are not too appealing either. Parents ask themselves if it is better for the children to be without both parents for part of the day or to be totally without daddy during all their waking hours.

It is a complex problem and one not easily solved, but in many cases there is a third option which is frequently overlooked. Why not have the full-time homemaker who wishes to stay at home continue to do so but make money at the same time? No, this is not some impossible dream. It is both practical and possible.

How Do I Get Started?

The first prerequisite required for successfully making money at home is to make up your mind to do so. As I explained in my book *Money in the Cookie Jar: The Christian Homemaker's Guide to Making Money at Home,* a home business will work only if the homemaker has fully determined that this course of action is right for her and that it meets the approval of God and her family.

First, realize there is nothing unscriptural about a woman having her own business. The virtuous woman in Proverbs 31 is our role model and she had a successful enterprise going on in a spare room of her house. Proverbs 31:24 says, "She maketh fine linen, and selleth it; and delivereth girdles unto the merchant."

The would-be entrepreneur of today should set priorities. Verse 15 of Proverbs 31 says of the virtuous woman: "She riseth also while it is yet night, and giveth meat to her household, and a portion to her maidens." Like this businesswoman, today's Christian homemaker needs to attend to both her spiritual and household duties before undertaking additional tasks.

The second matter to attend to before trying to make money at home is to make certain the cooperation of the entire family is enlisted. Even though a home business is less demanding in many ways than is going out to work, it is still a business and must be treated as one. This means that the family must be recruited to participate in household chores just as they would if the homemaker were going out to work. It also means that the project should meet with the approval of the husband. No matter what means of making money at home you choose, it will, to a great extent, affect each member of the family. If your husband is opposed to the idea, it is best to know in advance so that you can make other plans rather than finding out his feelings after you have invested time and maybe even cash into your fledgling enterprise. It would be unrealistic to think a home business could be conducted without making any ripples at all in the family routine. It is not possible to take from three to six hours a day out of your schedule and still be able to do all the things you were doing previously.

What Kind of Home Business Can I Start?

Sometimes it is difficult to decide what kind of approach to take in finding a way to make money at home. It might help if you first notice that all possible choices lie within three categories: teaching, service, or selling. Yet within each framework exists a multitude of possibilities.

Selling is a money-making choice that seems to appeal to most homemakers. Since most of us have learned to create various objects for the beautification of our own homes and wardrobes, it seems a simple matter to create more as a money-making project. As you think about the possibility of selling your handcrafted wares, consider a few things. Is there a market for what you will be creating? Find out *before* you make a hundred of them. Is the item as attractive and as well made as it can possibly be? Friends and relatives might buy a few of anything you make, but, if you want to be a success, you will have to impress strangers as well. What is the competition? If someone else is selling the same thing cheaper or in a wider selection of colors, you will need to know so that you can effectively compete. Consider that your competition does not come solely from other sellers. Sometimes a craft idea is so hot that everybody in town is learning to make that craft. You can't sell something everybody already knows how to make. Do you enjoy creating this item? It's dreadful to commit yourself to making five hundred items for the wholesaler, only to discover after the first dozen are finished that you thoroughly despise the whole process. Do you know how to treat your business as a business? It is important to keep your word about deadlines and delivery dates. Since others will be counting on you, be sure you can keep your word or else give up the idea of making money with your crafts.

Service jobs are those in which you do not create a product but rather take care of something belonging to someone else. Under the category of service jobs would be such things as dog grooming, shirt laundering, baby-sitting, clock repairing, or typing. Service jobs present a unique set of problems. You do not have complete control over the method to be used in the service job. Instead, you must perform your task in accordance with the preference of your customer. Consequently, if you are a creative person or one with firm ideas of how things are to be done, you might find yourself somewhat frustrated by a service job. If, however, you can follow directions and can enthusiastically perform a task in the manner your customer specifies, a service job might be just right for you.

Teaching is an option frequently overlooked by homemakers who want to make extra money at home. The idea of teaching might be a bit scary if you approach it in a traditional manner, but who says teaching has to be done that way? Children aren't the only ones who need teaching, classrooms aren't the only places to teach, and academic subjects are not the only courses in demand. Recreation centers constantly need people to teach crocheting, karate, cake decorating, and china painting. For this kind of teaching you don't even need a high school diploma, much less a college degree. There is also the possibility of lessons on a one-to-one basis. When I had a home sewing business I was frequently asked to "tutor" beginning seamstresses. Almost any subject which can be taught to a classroom full of people can be taught to just one person at a time, so shyness need not prevent your consideration of teaching.

Within these three categories lie a great many possibilities. Frequently it is possible to take one interest and use it to make money in all three ways. Let's take as an example, quilting. If this is your interest you might think first of making quilts to sell. However, because of the time involved in this you might conclude that quilting is not too feasible as a moneymaker because you can't complete a quilt fast enough to show any real profit. The usual thing that happens in a case like this is that the homemaker reluctantly discards the idea of making money with a hobby she truly loves and turns instead to something she is not too enthusiastic about rather than looking for alternate ways of making money with the thing she loves doing. For instance, for the quilter, there are several possibilities besides direct selling. She might turn to a *service* business in which she repairs old quilts or even provides customized laundry service. Or if that doesn't appeal to her, she might contact the recreation center or the senior citizen's groups or the local college or even an area fabric shop to see if the idea of quilting classes might be a feasible one. Thus, from one hobby has evolved three ideas for making money with three different categories of home businesses. Try to use this same evaluation method for the business you are contemplating.

Taking Care of Legal Requirements and Tax Responsibilities

Since my book *Money in the Cookie Jar* was published I have had the opportunity to talk to many women who are interested in making money at home, and the one thing all of them have in common is a fear of not knowing how to do the right thing in regard to legal requirements. Actually, there is not that much "legal stuff" involved in starting a home business. What you will need is a business license which is available from your city hall or county court house. This is fairly inexpensive and gives you the legal right to conduct a business at your home address. A lot of people don't bother to get this license, but as Christians we have the responsibility to set an example of obedience to the law.

The next thing you will need if you will be buying wholesale supplies or if you will be collecting sales tax on your merchandise (which is a requirement in retail selling) is a tax identification number. Simply contact the treasurer's office of your state capital and request the appropriate forms. This is no more complicated than is applying for a Social Security number.

The next step is to know what income tax forms you will need to fill out. In addition to your regular 1040 form you will need three others: form 1040 C, form 1040 SE, and form 1040 ES. For more information contact the nearest office of the Internal Revenue Service and ask for a free copy of their publication, *Tax Guide for Small Businesses*.

Of course, part of your time will be spent in record keeping. It is a *must* that you have an accurate account of your expenses and income. Many business-related expenses are tax deductions, and you don't want to miss out on anything you are legally entitled to deduct. Business supplies, equipment depreciation, car mileage for business purposes, postage costs, subscriptions to business-related magazines and newspapers, membership dues for professional organizations, and home office are just a few of the things you may be able to use to lower your tax burden. (Check with a qualified certified public accountant for the specifics of your case.) One of the best ways to keep accurate records is to set up a separate checking account for your business. Thus you can readily determine what expenses are involved and how much salary you have paid yourself.

If you are thinking about putting up signs to advertise your home business, check the zoning laws in your area first. Just because you are able to obtain a business permit and legally operate a business from your home does not mean that you have the freedom to display advertising. Find out about this *before* you hire a sign painter.

Finally, if you are involved with a food product, don't start selling it until you have it cleared with the health department. Food items carry more restrictions on their manufacture and sale than do most other homemade goods and you will need to inquire about any possible health examinations, kitchen inspections, or ingredients approval before you start your enterprise.

"I Need Some Cash—Quick!"

Sooner or later it happens. We find ourselves in a situation where an unexpected dental appointment or a car repair job or some other kind of financial emergency puts us in a temporarily binding situation. For times like that, a home business might not be feasible. After all, it does take a certain amount of time to get a home business going, and you might not have the necessary cash to buy raw materials to work with. The solution? Make some money in a hurry!

Garage sales are popular and profitable. Couldn't you acquire enough "junk" to go into business for one day? It is amazing how much unused material is lying around in our homes. Such things as books, furniture, children's clothes, games, and toys are good sellers. If you don't have enough merchandise to make a garage sale feasible for you, get together several friends and combine your treasures to come up with enough items to hold a successful sale. Another alternative is to allow others to place items in your sale with the agreement that they do not have to work at the sale but must pay you a percentage of the profits in exchange for your selling their goods.

Another quick source of cash is in recyclable products such as corrugated cardboard or aluminum cans. It takes a long time to acquire enough of this to sell if you depend on your own family as the supplier, but returns can be quick if you think like a businesswoman. Is there a grocery store in your area that would let you haul away the boxes they are planning to burn? It doesn't cost anything to ask. Is there a service station or an amusement park that would allow you to empty trash cans and claim the aluminum soft drink cans? Many of them are glad to be relieved of carting them away and will be glad to let you do the honors instead. To sell your recyclables, look in the business pages of the telephone book under the heading of "waste products" or "recyclable products."

If you live in an area where harvesting wild nuts, berries, or ornamental items is permissible, these products can also be the source of some quick funds. Many people enjoy eating nuts or berries but don't enjoy harvesting them. Many florists like to use natural materials such as pine cones, cattails, and natural grasses, and depend on independent workers like you to supply their needs.

The Care and Feeding of the Homemaker

Who Do You Love?

How do you feel about the homemaker in your home? (That's *you* we're talking about!)

Do you have feelings of inferiority or low self-esteem? Many homemakers do. Yet you have one of the most important jobs in the world. There is no need to feel unworthy because of your career. Certainly there are times when homemaking is neither exciting nor glamorous, but that might also be true of the job of the president of the United States.

As Christians we have an obligation to improve our self-image. After all, our bodies are the temples of the Holy Spirit, and, if we downgrade ourselves, aren't we being less than respectful to the One who dwells within us?

Yes, Christians are admonished to have humility, but they are also admonished to love themselves in the proper manner. Leviticus 19:18 commands, ". . . thou shalt love thy neighbor as thyself . . . ." If you don't have much enthusiasm about yourself, that which is reserved for your neighbor is not going to be of much significance either since your feelings about yourself are the measuring stick by which your love for others is gauged.

But this is not self-pride or conceit that we are talking about. The kind of self-love that is needed is not a selfish "me first" attitude but rather an outward reflection of God's love within you. This kind of love is sufficient to draw others to you and cause them to love you too. Have you ever noticed that it is the confident and outgoing person who seems to attract the most people to her side?

This is the essence of the whole idea. Once you see yourself as a worthwhile person who is doing a worthwhile job as a homemaker, you can forget self and concentrate on others. Hard as it may be to believe, feelings of inferiority are actually a form of conceit! Rather than leaving others free to be themselves, the woman with low self-esteem seems to cry out for constant attention to bolster her poor, tender feelings. Her whole attitude conveys the message, "Look at me. I'm not worth much, am I?" Instead of putting self aside she is constantly exalting herself, because no matter where she goes or what she does her thoughts are of herself.

It is only when a homemaker accepts herself as God's creation who exists exactly according to His specifications, can she move on to matters beyond herself. Having learned to love a crooked nose or a pair of squinty eyes just because God selected them for you, immediately moves mere looks out of the forefront and leaves you free to get on to more important things. Have you been guilty of downgrading God's creation?

Beauty Is Only Skin Deep?

I doubt if anyone of my generation managed to grow up without being told at least once that "beauty is only skin deep" or "pretty is as pretty does." Both statements are obviously true but that is not much consolation when your face is covered with acne or your home permanent has frizzed.

Yet what lies within you is the best beauty treatment you

will ever give yourself. Do you have the joy that goes with being a Christian? If so, then even sallow or less than perfect complexions can achieve a glow. Do you have the peace of knowing that whatever comes your way, God is in charge of your life? If so, your face will reflect a serenity that cannot be achieved with tranquilizers. Do you awake each morning with enthusiasm for the day the Lord has given you? If so, your eyes will sparkle and even if they are small or short-lashed they can still be your most expressive feature.

This kind of beauty is the best kind. It doesn't depend for its existence on jars or bottles or ample budgets. Instead, it radiates from within and makes the outside more attractive. Living the joyful life of a Christian makes any woman beautiful.

Then there is the matter of actions. Even the most gorgeously attired beauty is not appealing to look at when her face is lined with worry or anger. What is inside spills over to destroy the perfection of a physically beautiful, immaculately-groomed woman if her thoughts are ugly.

Even though "pretty is as pretty does" is certainly true, and that God looks on the heart instead of the outward appearance is equally true, it seems some Christian women have taken these thoughts to excess. Have you ever seen a woman whose spirituality was not for a moment in question, but whose personal appearance tended to drive people away from her? It is not likely that a woman will be much of a witness for Christ if her outward appearance is such that onlookers can only think, "I certainly don't want to be like her!" While God is indeed looking on the heart, people are looking on the outward appearance and forming opinions.

When I was a child we lived in a small town, and near our house was a church which differed considerably from our own. I can remember being so very glad that my parents were not of that denomination. Since I was too young then to understand about spiritual matters, I probably saw those Christian women in an erroneous way and, as a consequence, misjudged them. It wasn't just the lack of make-up or of brightly-colored clothing that I noticed the most.

Rather it was the more general feeling of unconcern about looks. Then, as now, I failed to understand how sagging hemlines, dirty fingernails, and greasy hair could serve as a spiritual barometer. Even if a woman's religious convictions prevent her from cutting her hair or wearing make-up, she can still be well groomed.

Although an obsession with grooming is not appropriate for the Christian woman, taking good care of the vessel God has created is just another form of stewardship. If God gave you an object which He had handcrafted exactly to His specifications would you treat it in just any old way or would you give it the care and attention it deserved? In the same way He has given us our bodies as the "packaging" for the Holy Spirit, and we have no business mistreating the container or purposely making it unattractive!

In I Peter 3:3-4 we are warned about an overconcern for external matters. It is possible to take concern for looks to an outrageous extreme, and this is the situation Peter is warning against. But the Bible offers no condemnation of the appropriate kind of beauty. Some of the best-known women of the Bible were well dressed, nicely groomed, and probably quite beautiful.

Sarah was so beautiful that at the time she was sixty-four years old, her looks were still remarkable. "And it came to pass, that when Abram was come into Egypt, the Egyptians beheld the woman that she was very fair" (Gen. 12:14). Somehow, I have a hard time imagining "senior citizen" Sarah having lanky hair and a potbelly if she had that kind of effect on those who saw her!

Esther was a woman whose beauty—both physical and spiritual—were the means by which a nation was saved from death. The Bible describes Esther as "fair and beautiful" (Esther 2:7). Can you imagine her having the same devastating effect on King Ahasuerus if she had set about to influence him while wearing hair curlers, beach sandals, and paint-stained jeans? True, Esther's spiritual beauty was her greatest asset, but Ahasuerus didn't know anything about that because "man looks on the outside."

Is Homemaking Just Any Old Job?

Just for a few minutes let's travel to a city park bench to do some people watching. First, you see a group of nurses strolling together on a shopping trip during their lunch hour. You probably notice the professionalism and good grooming those spotless white uniforms convey. Then there are the secretaries, who are young and quite style conscious. Watching them is a good opportunity for learning what is "in" as far as fashion goes. Next come the women executives. They dress in conservative suits and carry small handbags.

These three groups of women don't seem to have much in common when you begin comparing appearances, but, in spite of the differences in dress, one fact is apparent: each one recognizes the importance of her position and, as a result her facial expression, manner of dress, and even her walk convey her pride in her station in life.

Then there are the homemakers. Let's move from that city park bench to a suburban shopping mall. It is my guess that you won't have to wait long to see a young mother in hair curlers with not a hint of color on her face and wearing her husband's cast-off shirt. *This* is a representative of the most important career in the world? No wonder so many two-career homemakers look disdainfully on the thought of being "just a housewife."

Homemaking is as much a worthwhile career as is any other and it is incomprehensible to me that so many one-career homemakers can't seem to take the same interest in looks as do their two-career homemaker friends.

The homemaker's "dress for success" plan need not make a big dent in the family budget. Clothing doesn't have to be expensive or of the latest fashion. What it does need to be is right for your figure and your lifestyle. Then it needs to be kept in good order—washed, ironed, and mended as necessary. The idea of wearing just any old piece of clothing "around the house" needs to be rethought. That is your family you are dressing for. Would you look different if you knew the president were coming for dinner? Of course! Yet, who in your lifetime will ever be as precious to you as your husband

and children? Don't they deserve someone pretty to look at too?

It takes only a few minutes to run a comb through your hair, to apply a dash of lipstick, and to put on a dab of perfume. The psychological effect created by your actions will give you a boost of self-esteem which will greatly improve your entire day.

Puff! Pant! Ouch!

Exercise might be defined as the "lubricant" that helps to keep our joints and muscles working effectively. Therefore, if we expect to glide into old age instead of creaking into it, we have to exercise.

The problem is that most of us would rather not exercise. Add to this lack of enthusiasm a lack of available time—which is the standard excuse we all use when we would rather not do a particular thing that we ought to do. How then can we keep our bodies healthy and fit with a minimum of time and an absence of enthusiasm?

One disguise for exercise is sports activity. Maybe the idea of knee bends doesn't appeal to you, but a twice weekly game of tennis might be more fun than you suspect. Likewise, a brisk run around the block might be boring, but a long walk with one of your children accomplishes the same results with the added bonus of giving you an opportunity to communicate with your child on an individual basis.

I get bored when I try to impose a fifteen-minute exercise period on myself but I don't feel bored at all when I break it down into several segments. After a few hours at the typewriter, a minute or so of jumping rope gets me limbered up and helps me to think better when I return to work. All kinds of exercise can be slipped into a day without setting aside a large block of time for that purpose. Try running in place for a minute after you finish making the bed or do twenty sit-ups after the breakfast dishes have been washed.

Everyday activities can be used as exercise too. Take the stairs instead of the elevator if you have a choice. At home you might try making one or two extra trips up and down the stairs several times a day. Or volunteer to rake the leaves in the church yard. Or walk a dog for a neighbor who is ill.

Hey! Exercise isn't so bad, after all, is it?

"But I'm So Tired!"

If there is one thing homemakers have in common, it is tiredness. Most of us, particularly those with small children, find our days are filled with constant activity. It is hard to have a sparkling radiance about you when you are so tired all the time that your idea of a big evening is one in which you get to sleep by nine o'clock.

For the homemaker who is serious about giving her family the best, the starting point is herself. How can anybody be patient, understanding, efficient, well organized, and attractive when she is so tired that she can't get her thoughts in order?

Do you know *why* you are so tired? It is not possible to cure a problem without first diagnosing it. Most cases of fatigue fall into four categories: physical problems, mental problems, lack of proper sleep or rest, and actual overwork.

The most obvious of these categories is overwork, but in talking to other women about this I don't find too many who define overwork as the culprit in their tiredness. After all, most of us don't have to plow the south forty acres before breakfast or scrub all the clothes on a scrubbing board each wash day. Most cases of overwork tiredness are not from actual overwork but from contributing causes such as improper work habits, poor planning, or too much of a sense of perfectionism. Some women do have too heavy a schedule, but the majority who complain of having too much to do can alleviate much of the problem by being organized and by learning to slow down and relax a bit.

Then there is the matter of mental problems. Depression has been called an epidemic in this country. It is hard to keep your outlook cheery when it costs so much to buy groceries or when the car is constantly in the shop or when your husband has to work two jobs just to make a living. But worry is not constructive. Rather than worry, why not sit down in a quiet spot and plan ways of dealing with your moods. Check your diet to see if you are eating properly. Too many sweets can cause depression. Try an exercise program. It is hard to be depressed when you are struggling for breath! Most of all, try turning your thoughts away from yourself and your problems. One sure way to lift your spirits is by doing a deed that will lift someone else's. If none of these ideas work for you have your doctor check for physical reasons for your tiredness and depression.

In spite of all the jokes about "tired blood" it is a fact that many young women are anemic. This happened to me one time, and I couldn't understand why it was such an effort to get myself out of bed each morning and drag myself through my daily chores. Finally, my husband insisted that I see a doctor, and I was told my blood count was low. With the proper medicine I was feeling perky again in a few weeks. Of course, other physical ailments that are somewhat less common may also be the culprit in your tiredness. It doesn't hurt to check with your doctor if the fatigue just won't go away. Homemakers don't get sick leave so we have to try to stay as healthy as possible.

Particularly for young mothers, the major factor contributing to perpetual tiredness may be a lack of sleep. Eight hours between going to bed and shutting off the alarm may not give you enough sleep, particularly if you have to get up four or five times during that eight hours to take care of the children's needs. The solution? Get enough rest even if you have to give up your favorite television program or your bowling night or mopping the kitchen floor. If the children take a nap in the afternoon it might be a good idea to take one with them. You and your family are both shortchanged when inadequate rest makes you less than your best.

Are You a Workaholic?

At a gathering I attended recently a group of women were discussing the meticulous housekeeping done by another member of the group who was not present.

"Her floors are so clean you could eat off them!" came the predictable comment.

Several others chimed in to discuss the other attributes of this model housekeeper. Then finally someone said to the sister of the woman being discussed, "I suppose you are just as efficient a housekeeper as your sister."

"I hope not!" was the fervent reply. "I wouldn't want to know my husband had to go to a relative's house to watch football, take his shoes off, and eat snacks in the living room."

Isn't the whole idea of homemaking to provide a place of comfort and refuge for the family members? Something is wrong when home ceases to be a place in which family members can relax and be themselves—and frequently the "something that is wrong" is that the homemaker is a workaholic.

Many homemakers are workaholics and don't even know it. As a matter of fact, we have all become so conditioned to those horrible cartoons which portray the homemaker as an overweight frump in hair curlers and a tattered bathrobe, that it is hard for us to realize that some women go to the other extreme and expect too much perfection. Just like their workaholic counterpart in the world of science or medicine or business, they reach a point where work is the all-consuming ideal. Instead of looking for easier methods of housekeeping, they delight in finding more and more chores to add to the list. In fact, they become so engrossed in housekeeping that they no longer have time for picnics or for an evening of television with the family or for an hour spent reading to a child or perhaps even for going to church.

There are several varieties of workaholics, so they are not always as easy to spot as might be imagined. For some it is not just housework that drives them but other things as well. Do you know a homemaker who gives every job she does everything she can throw into it? Even when she "relaxes" she does it at an unrelenting pace.

Then there is the workaholic that reminds you of a corn popper throwing kernels out in all directions. She is probably a "superwoman" who keeps a spotless house, participates in every church activity, bakes her own bread, finds time to be a Pink Lady and president of the P.T.A. and makes every other woman within twenty-five miles feel inadequate by comparison.

Next, there is the woman who "puts all her eggs in one basket." All her chores are domestic ones but she goes all out to keep an immaculate house, grow a garden, make all her Christmas gifts, and so on. She doesn't go out as much as the "superwoman" does but she creates quite a whirlwind in the small area she does occupy.

Last, of course, is the workaholic we all know. She doesn't garden or sew or bake bread. She cleans and cleans and cleans. She can't relax for a moment. She sees dirt before it's there and wipes fingerprints off the counter before the finger that goes with them can move out of the way.

Are you a workaholic? If so, re-examine your motives and priorities and commit your housekeeping to the Lord. He can cure a case of compulsive housekeeping just as surely as He can cure any other malady, and the result will be a great deal of happiness added to your home.

"I Need a Vacation!"

My husband is a government employee. Because of this his vacation allotment is not measured in days or weeks but in hours. He can—if his boss is agreeable to it—take an hour's "vacation," which is then subtracted off his total annual leave for the year. This system is quite handy.

Wouldn't it be nice if homemakers could occasionally take an hour-long vacation? Well, why can't we?

In an hour you can: take a leisurely soak in the bathtub, write a letter to a friend, take the dog for a walk, plant a row of flowers, read a few chapters in a book, lie outdoors in the chaise lounge and take a nap, or even catch up on all the long, chatty telephone calls you have been wanting to make.

Jesus recognized that human bodies need the occasional recharge of vacations. He said to His followers, "Come ye yourselves apart into a desert place, and rest a while . . ." (Mark 6:31). Our bodies aren't made for perpetual motion, and the time "lost" to an hour's vacation might be the best investment you will make all day in getting more accomplished.

But I Don't Have a Thing to Wear!

Your Closet Runneth Over?

Have you ever wondered why it is that the more clothing a person owns, the more difficult it seems to find something to wear? All across the country men, women, and children, with closets jammed full, are wailing, "But I don't have anything to wear!"

We buy more clothing than any generation that ever lived, yet, unlike Grandma who had one Sunday best dress and knew precisely what she would wear for every special occasion, many of us never seem to achieve the finished look Grandma had. Many women are letting their clothes closet manage them rather than vice versa.

Proverbs 31:10-31 gives us a role model to follow to be the best possible homemaker. The virtuous woman described in these verses had her life organized and running smoothly. Despite her many household duties, charity activities, and spiritual priorities, this woman found time to dress well. Four of the twenty-two verses which describe this role model discuss some aspect of clothing preparation. Nearly one-fifth of what we are told about the woman is in some way connected with the making or wearing of clothing.

This virtuous woman lovingly made practical garments (wool and flax are mentioned in verse 13 and winter clothing is mentioned in verse 21) and elegant ones. This woman was no shrinking violet who wore only basic black. Look at verse 22: "She maketh herself coverings of tapestry; her clothing is silk and purple." It would be rather difficult to ignore somebody dressed like that!

Yet the real lesson of Proverbs 31 is that spiritual priorities come first. Verse 22 is the only verse in the chapter that dwells exclusively on the outward appearance of the virtuous woman. All the other verses tell of her diligence, her good works, her spiritual attributes, her capability in household tasks, and her care of her family. Only one verse is given over to the description of her clothing. Her apparel was magnificent—and costly—but it wasn't high on this woman's list of priorities. Many household duties took precedence over the making of fine apparel.

Another factor in this woman's make-up was her concern for her family's clothing needs. The rest of the family had clothing that was serviceable, appropriate, and elegant as the occasion required. Somehow it seems inconceivable that this woman's family had closets jammed with "white elephants."

How to Get Started

Nothing is more frustrating than trying to get dressed in a hurry, only to discover that your husband's last clean white shirt is missing a button, that your son's only pair of socks that still have both heels and toes in them are lime green, and that you can't wear your new orange dress because you don't own a pair of shoes that doesn't clash with that shade of orange. Does this sound like Sunday morning at your house?

The basic goal to strive toward is not a full closet but rather a workable wardrobe. If you inform your husband that you've made the decision to revamp the entire family's wardrobe, you'll probably need to revive him with the smelling salts. The strategy I'm going to propose for creating a workable wardrobe, however, doesn't involve expense as much as it does common sense.

For several years I had a dressmaking business in my home. During that time I sewed for many families. The thing that most impressed me about well-dressed women was not how much money they spent on clothing, but how they planned and coordinated their wardrobes to get maximum mileage from each garment they owned.

Already I can hear somebody groaning, "That's fine for them, but what do I do with the clothes I already own?" I can't afford to throw everything out and start over."

Most of us couldn't afford such drastic measures and that is why I'm not about to suggest such a thing. Rather, let's start with the garments the family already owns and proceed from there. The first step is inventory. Take note of colors, fabrics, wearability, personal tastes, and lifestyle.

Does your closet contain your high school cheerleading costume and your husband's football sweater? Get them out of the closet and into the attic or basement.

Does your daughter's closet contain clothing she outgrew two years ago. Give it away, put it in a garage sale, or recycle it for her younger sister.

Does your son's chest of drawers still contain that pair of orange striped pajamas your great aunt gave him three years ago? Get them out and turn them into dusting cloths. (Some clothing should not even be dumped on the Goodwill Industries or the Salvation Army!)

Does your husband's wardrobe contain undershirts with air vents and socks without heels? He is not going to wear those things, so why leave them in the drawer where he has to sort through them every morning?

After clearing out the unwearables, it is quite likely that you will be surprised at what is left. It may be that you will even turn up some desirable items you had forgotten were pushed into the back of the closet.

The next step after sorting through all the drawers and

closets is to coordinate what is left. A garment is a white elephant if it doesn't go with anything else. These things don't belong in your wardrobe unless you can plan an inexpensive purchase of another item to make the white elephant usable. But be careful: it is worthwhile to buy one thing in order to make a garment useful again. It is not worthwhile to keep the white elephant if you are going to need shoes, bag, and another garment in order to make the orphan useful again.

The third step in coordinating your wardrobe lies in removing all the items in need of mending. If you have been letting this go undone for a while, things may look discouraging, but unless all those unwearable garments are pulled out of the closets and drawers and put in a visible spot, they are never going to get mended.

The final step in this wardrobe analysis is to repair the worthwhile garments and get them back into the closet as soon as possible so that you can more accurately determine what new purchases are needed. Then you will be ready to begin the next phase of revamping your wardrobe.

Getting Down to Basics

One of the most useful ways to create a workable wardrobe is to let everything revolve around one basic color. In this way you can more easily coordinate everything you own. Of course, the selection of this basic color is strictly a matter of personal preference. Navy blue is my choice, but brown, black, gray, or green might work just as well for you. The goal is to select a color around which all other colors in your wardrobe can revolve. This does not limit your choices, but rather expands them. By choosing a somewhat neutral starting point, you wind up with all colors of the rainbow to coordinate with that basic choice.

For instance, my choice of navy blue might sound drab to you, but those who know me would readily admit that drab colors are not my style at all. Suppose I have a navy blue skirt and I decide to buy a new blouse to go with it. I can choose pastel blue, bright red, a floral print, stripes of any width, or polka dots of any size.

After choosing the basic color around which a wardrobe is to be built, the next step is to choose shoes and handbags to go with it. Nothing ruins the finished look of a well-groomed woman faster than does the wrong shoes and bag. Yet it is not at all necessary to own a shoe rack full of shoes in order to look well-dressed. The important thing is to start with the color that best suits the basic color scheme you have chosen and to then add other sets of shoes and purses to it as you have the additional finances. If I were just starting to build my wardrobe around navy blue, my first purchase would be navy blue shoes and a matching purse. Then, as funds permitted, I might add red shoes or white ones or whatever else seems appropriate.

One of the best ways to build a basic wardrobe is by choosing separates that can be changed to create a variety of looks. Skirts, blouses, and jackets can be coordinated so that it is not always necessary to wear the same blouse with the same skirt, and in this way much more mileage is achieved from the clothing dollar. If you are just beginning to put together your new coordinated wardrobe, try starting with one basic skirt and matching jacket. Then add several blouses that can be used to change the appearance of the suit. Next you might want to add another skirt that will go with the same jacket and blouses. By gradually adding garments as you can afford them, you will eventually have an entire wardrobe of coordinated garments.

One of the best ways to take advantage of sales while still sticking with the basic wardrobe plan is to carry fabric samples with you when you shop. If you sew, cut a small scrap of fabric and tuck it into your purse when you go to a sale, so that you won't have to wonder if that sale-priced sweater will match your skirt.

Of course, coordinating a wardrobe does take time. It would be a financially fortunate woman who could make such a switch in less than a year, and, if finances are really tight, two years may be a more realistic estimate of the time needed for the switchover. The important thing to remember is that, in the long run, having a workable wardrobe will result in less total expenditures for clothing since everything in it matches everything else. Therefore, it is worth striving for the coordinated effect even if it does take quite a while to achieve it.

How to Shop for Clothing

Throughout the years I have learned a few workable shortcuts that help make clothes shopping easier for me. I'll pass them on for you to try:

1. *Know what you are looking for.* By defining precisely what need a garment is to serve, you can more accurately pinpoint what you are looking for. Is the white blouse you are seeking for dressup or for casual wear? Are the shoes you are buying strictly for use with a tailored suit or will buying a slightly lower heel make them feasible also for wearing with your favorite wrap-around skirt?

2. *Know the alternatives.* As you shop, ask yourself, "What can I substitute if this item is not available?" Take note of the alternatives while you are in each store. Then after visiting five or six stores without successfully locating the item you sought, you will know which store to return to in order to acquire the best alternative.

3. *Plan ahead.* It's better to start thinking about buying shoes when you see the thin spot in your daughter's sneakers instead of waiting until the day her toes come poking through. By keeping a constant inventory of your family's wardrobe, you can start to look for needed items before something turns into a "have-to" situation.

4. *Shop cooperatively.* Your shopping time is cut considerably if you know before you walk into a store that what you need is there. Work out a cooperative plan with a few of your friends. While one of them is buying her son's western boots, she can ask if the store has your son's size and color in the jogging shoes you have been seeking. While you are buying your husband a brown wallet for his birthday, notice whether the store also carries the black trifold style one of your friends

108

wants to buy. A bargain network can help everybody save money. Have an agreement with your friends that whoever finds bargains on anything that all of you buy frequently will immediately telephone the rest of the group with the news. This makes it possible for all of you to cover more territory in less time.

5. *Know quality.* There was a time when price was the primary indicator of quality, but this is no longer true. As a seamstress, I was amazed when I examined some of the poor-quality, high-priced garments my customers brought to me for alteration work. Price alone is not the determining factor in choosing quality garments. Quality is a combination of fabric choice, appropriate design, ample cut, and skilled construction techniques.

Judging Quality

Do you sew? If you do, then perhaps, like me, you are aware of the inferior quality of some ready-made garments. It is disappointing to pay a hefty price for a piece of clothing, only to have the hem come undone with the first washing or the neckline facings poke out because they were not properly sewn down. Here are some guidelines for buying quality clothing for the family:

1. *Is the fabric suitable for the pattern?* Home sewing enthusiasts are not the only ones who make the mistake of matching the wrong fabric and pattern. Sometimes clothing designers do this too, and the result is a lowering of the overall quality of the garment.

2. *Is the fabric cut well?* It is possible to sew up a ripped seam but it is not possible for any seamstress to correct the poor fit of a badly-cut garment. No matter how beautiful a design might be or how appealing a bargain price might seem, a garment is not a good buy if it is not cut well. The garment must be cut with the grain of the fabric or it will never hang properly at the hemline. In addition, the sleeves

109

should not bind when the arms are lifted, the waistline should be precisely at the waist, and the skirt should not crawl up when you walk. For long sleeves, proper fit means that the sleeves cover the wristbone. For skirts, particularly bias cut ones, proper fit means an even hem and a grain line that does not cause the skirt to sag at the hipline.

3. *Is the garment constructed well?* Ample seam allowances used to be one of the marks of quality, but now even some of the better-known clothing manufacturers are starting to skimp on seam allowances. It is advisable, however, to buy garments with a half-inch or more of seam allowance when you can find them at a price you can afford, because otherwise no alterations will be possible if you gain a few pounds or if the garment shrinks when it is washed.

Another construction point to check is the stitching. Seams should be sewn with about twelve stitches to the inch. If a garment has less than that, it is not going to hold together well, and you will constantly be restitching ripped places. Give a tug on the back seam of trousers and slacks if these are going to be bought to fit snugly. If so, choose a brand that features stretch stitches that give under pressure; this saves a lot of embarrassment in the long run. Stay away from garments that are sewn with colorless nylon thread. It is scratchy against the skin and, while it doesn't break easily, it does tend to come unsewn.

Zippers and other fasteners are important too. When buying men's trousers choose those with metal zippers rather than nylon ones. After a few washings, the nylon ones tend to separate while the garment is being worn. It is getting more and more difficult to find women's garments with metal zippers. But whenever you do have a choice, the metal ones are the most durable.

When inspecting trousers, be particularly choosy about pockets. Look for pockets that are made of sturdy material, even if you are buying a suit rather than a pair of casual slacks. Men carry almost as much weight in their pockets—even when they are dressed up—as we carry in our purses, so those pockets need to be durable. Learn to recognize those that contain rayon (it ravels) or dacron (it "pills"). Check, too, for ample belt loops. Nothing detracts from a man's well-dressed appearance faster than does a gap between his belt and his waistband.

4.   Is the style a basic one or a faddish one? The woman who wants to get the most for her clothing dollar will avoid the clothing fads that come and go. Quality clothing should be virtually timeless. Just because some of the Paris designers are putting spangles and feathers on their five-thousand-dollar dresses does not mean that those dresses have quality as far as lasting wearability is concerned. A basic garment of good quality construction should be as stylish next year as it is this year.

How to Achieve the Custom Look

If you know how to sew your family's clothing, you are already on your way to achieving the custom look in your clothing. But even if you don't sew everything from scratch, you can do basic sewing that can make all the difference between the bargain rack look and the quality look. Even a ready-made garment can be improved.

For instance, look at the hems and zippers in some of your favorite ready-made garments. Even those with a name brand tag are probably not as nicely done as they would have been if they had been custom sewn by a competent dressmaker. With little effort you can give your family's clothing that special touch. Simply take out the machine-stitched hem and zipper and redo them by hand. Nothing says "custom" faster than an invisibly hemmed skirt and a hand-sewn zipper.

Another improvement you might want to add is in the facings. Most are not sewn down and tend to work out as the garment is worn. A few stitches will anchor the facings and make the article of clothing look finished. You may want to add hooks and eyes at stress points. Ready-made garments frequently lack these touches, and a few minutes spent sewing can add considerably to the quality look of the garment.

One or two nicely monogrammed articles in your wardrobe can add a distinctive touch, and this can be done easily to ready-made clothing. Just don't get over enthused with the idea, or what started out as a mark of distinction will appear to be just another gimmick. If your sewing machine doesn't have a monogramming attachment, it is possible to monogram freehand if you can draw attractive letters and your sewing machine will do a satin stitch.

On children's clothing nothing says "specialty shop" faster than touches of embroidery or applique. These can be done by hand and should be rather small. If you aren't an artist, trace a simple design such as a duck or train or sailboat from a child's coloring book.

Even if you don't know how to hem or to put in invisibly sewn zippers or to monogram or to applique, you can still customize your new outfit. Simply remove the inexpensive plastic buttons and replace them with more appropriate ones of the same size. If the skirt of the dress or suit is too long and you are going to have someone shorten it for you, ask her to return the cutoff fabric to you. With it you can make fabric-covered buttons which will greatly improve the special look of your new garment.

If you really want to improve the look of an inexpensive dress without doing any sewing at all, replace the cheap looking belt that came with the dress. Use a straw belt you already have in your closet or a contrasting leather belt you purchased to wear with a different outfit. A paisley silk scarf can be threaded through the belt loops of a skirt or pair of slacks. For casual summer wear try cord belts. Several strands of the cord used for clothesline can be purchased at the hardware and then knotted together for a casual look that is perfect with summer skirts.

Have you been discouraged because your small clothing budget prohibits you from buying the kind of quality clothing you would like to have? Then cheer up! With these customizing touches, you can have the finished look you'd like without increasing your clothing allowance at all.

Makin' Do

Waste Not, Want Not?

I've been told by people who lived through the depression years of the 1930s that one of the most frequently repeated bits of advice was, "Use it up. Wear it out. Make it do." During those days the idea of frugality and recycling were not optional. It was a case of learning to be clever with what you had or doing without.

One of the keys to good use of family money lies in learning to be less wasteful. Learning to make good use out of what we have is a form of stewardship. How can we, in good conscience, ask God to bless our family and supply its monetary needs when we are throwing our money into the garbage can as fast as we can cash our paychecks and spend them on unnecessary items?

"Waste not, want not" is truth in capsule form. Wise use of our goods is one of the best ways to show our stewardship. Because the homemaker is usually the family member most

113

responsible for cutting waste, it is important that we accept this discipline. The Bible says, ". . . a prudent wife is from the Lord."

Thriftiness in Action

According to the dictionary, thriftiness is a form of economical management. According to real life, thriftiness is saving money in one area so that we can enjoy spending it more profitably in another area.

Which is more enjoyable, failing to turn the water faucet completely off, thus raising the water bill by a dollar a month, which amounts to twelve dollars a year, or using that same twelve dollars to buy a special gift for someone or to pay for a lengthy call to a parent who lives in a faraway state?

Which is the most fun, buying groceries without taking time to bargain hunt, thus raising your grocery bill by $5 a week for a total of $260 a year, or using $260 to pay for your lodging at a vacation spot?

Thriftiness is not the selfish hoarding of money just for the sake of having it, but rather the conscious choosing to cut corners in one place in order to have funds for something more enjoyable.

Use It Up

Each item you buy is purchased with money that was given in exchange for a specified portion of your time. If you make ten dollars an hour, then every ten-dollar item you buy costs you one hour of your life. That puts wasting in a different perspective, doesn't it?

Yet some women routinely discard shirts with one missing button or trousers with a broken zipper or returnable bottles and cans or half-filled containers of cleaning products.

114

"Using it up" means that you will cut the top off the can of cleansing powder in order to get one more tub scrubbing from the powder that is left in the bottom. It also means using soap as long as the bar is still a bar, and then putting the fragments into a container to be used for handwashing lingerie.

"Using it up" could mean that you will wear a blouse until the cuffs start to fray and then cut the sleeves out to make a sleeveless blouse for wearing with your casual summer skirts. Then when the colors fade, you will put the blouse in the rag bag. (Nothing makes a better dustcloth than does an old, soft undershirt, and nothing is better for car washing than old terry cloth towels. Why buy disposable towels for these purposes?)

"Using it up" also means saving all those miscellaneous leftover vegetables and putting them into a pot of soup. It means being aware of that last, lonely potato left in the storage bin. Slice it into chunks and cook it with your green beans or dice it finely, cook it for a few minutes, and then combine it with chopped, leftover roast beef for a low-cost beef hash that is tasty at the breakfast table.

"Using it up" means never throwing away stale bread. It has a multitude of uses. Try it in bread pudding or as French toast. Put separated pieces of leftover hamburger or hot dog buns into a skillet with some butter and cook until the bottoms are buttery and toasted around the edges and the tops are soft and moist. These are delicious with breakfast. If you like crunchy salad toppings, turn your surplus stale bread into flavored accompaniments for your green salads. Grate some stale, solid bread into a skillet. Add a few pats of butter, some onion salt or garlic powder or parmesan cheese or some other herb, and stir the mixture as it cooks until it is a toasted golden color. The result is a crunchy salad topping.

"Using it up" means using leftover pie crust to make what I call "sort-of" cookies. Flatten small balls of the crust onto a cookie sheet, sprinkle with cinnamon and sugar, and bake at 350° until tan in color. These flaky cookies will probably be so popular that you will have to start making extra pie crust in order to fill the demand.

"Using it up" also means that you will use a lipstick brush to scoop out the last smidgen of color in the tube. When a lipstick tube goes into the trash can it should be only that—a tube. It also helps to use up all the lotion and all the deodorant rather than letting the last half ounce or so go to waste. By turning the bottle upside down overnight, the last drops will run down to the neck of the bottle by morning so that the final bit of roll-on deodorant can be utilized. In similar fashion, the last of the hand lotion will have collected in the bottle cap and can be scooped out and used.

"Using it up" means learning to utilize all leftover foods in a creative manner. One banana isn't enough to feed a family of four—unless you slice it into a gelatin mixture. At the end of Christmas holidays you might find yourself left with little bits of baking ingredients such as coconut and nuts. Or there might be a few odds and ends of fruit left lying in the fruit bowl. Combine one banana, two or three or even four oranges—whatever you have on hand—and an apple or two, those few spoonfuls of coconut, and a half cup or more of raw unsalted pecans or walnuts. The result is a fruit salad you can serve without apology as you thriftily rid your kitchen of all the holiday "orphans."

Wear It Out

When was the last time you threw away something that was truly worn out? For many homemakers the answer might be, "the last time I managed to sneak a pair of faded and ragged jeans out of my daughter's closet."

It is rare for us to wear anything out anymore. We start to dislike the color and we throw the garment out. We decide the style is hopelessly outdated and, instead of doing a remodeling job, we get rid of the garment. Of course, nobody wants to wear clothing that is faded or hopelessly dated in styling, but most of us do tend to be a little quick to

116

head toward the garbage can. Most garments have far more possibilities left in them than might be supposed. For instance, parts of two-piece suits wear out at different rates. Why not keep a good skirt even if its matching top is no longer wearable? If it was a carefully planned purchase and coordinates with the rest of the wardrobe, it probably still has some possibilities left in it.

Perhaps you can convert one garment into another. Suppose you have a pullover knit top that is torn in a conspicuous spot that makes mending it out of the question. Why not recycle it into a shirt for your small daughter or for your son if the color is right. It is not necessary to rip out seams. Just take a pair of scissors and cut the garment open along the sides near the seam lines, trim the sleeves away, and you have flat surfaces on which a pattern can be placed. If you are careful when you position the pattern, the old hem can be utilized for the new garment, and you won't even have to hem the "new" shirt.

Recycling adult clothing into children's clothing gives you more mileage for your clothing dollar. When hemlines drop drastically and you are left with a number of out-of-style skirts, it is simple to remake them for a daughter. Also, since pajama trousers tend to wear out faster than the matching tops, you might recycle your husband's pajama shirt into a shirt for his son. If the buttonholes are not too large, your "new" garment can be constructed in such a way that the original buttonholes can be utilized on the second garment.

Recycling is not just a matter of cutting down an adult-sized garment into a child-sized one. Sometimes it works in reverse as well. For instance, my daughter has outgrown a floor-length party skirt with silver thread in it. Next stop for that skirt is a bodice for a special dress I'm planning to make for myself. I'll need to purchase only enough white crepe or similar dressy fabric to make a skirt and I will have an elegant dress without spending much at all.

Another recycling possibility lies in converting one article in a child's wardrobe into something else. For example, when embroidered denim was "in," I embroidered a large design on the back of one of Karen's jackets. She has out-grown the jacket, but, since the embroidered design is still as colorful as ever, I plan to cut a square from the back of that jacket and recycle the design onto a bib-front jumper.

One of the reasons a lot of clothes aren't worn more is because the wearer grew out of them. There is not much you can do about size changes if you buy ready-made clothing. But if you sew your children's clothing, growth features can be built into any garment you make. A growth in height rather than an increase in weight is what makes most cloth-ing unwearable. The waistline, the hemline, and the sleeves show the first indications of a child's growth spurt. If you sew, add an extra inch of material at the waistline of a dress and make this into a tuck on the underside of the garment so that it can be let down at a later date. Generous hems help, too, but too large a hem may ruin the appearance of a gar-ment. Make a wide hem and then take one or two tucks on the underside of the hem. The result will be a generous hem that isn't conspicuously oversized.

In a similar fashion, girls' slips can be worn for a longer period of time if you buy the slip one size larger—exact fit is not quite as crucial in slips as in dresses—and then make a waistline tuck on the underside and a series of small, decora-tive tucks just above the hemline on the right side of the slip. Make the tucks small—about a half-inch of fabric in each one—and they will look like a decorative feature instead of an economy measure. As the child grows, the tucks can be snipped to provide the necessary extra length.

Sleeves with cuffs should be avoided when a child is grow-ing rapidly. A better alternative is to put an elastic casing at the end of your daughter's sleeve. If you make the kind with a fabric self-ruffle, the casing can be moved to the end of the sleeve as she grows. Later the sleeve can be shortened to a below-the-elbow style.

Most mothers have, at one time or another, used the trick of putting colorful rickrack trim over an old hemline in order to disguise the faded mark that was left when the hem was lowered. But this idea has limitations. If not done correctly it

118

looks quite obvious. A better solution than applying just one row of rickrack over the faded hemline is to apply two or three rows in various colors or sizes so that it looks as though you planned the decoration from the beginning of the garment's construction. Space the rickrack rows from a half-inch to an inch apart, depending on the size of the child. Then, using the smallest size of rickrack, repeat this row on either the edge of the collar or the hemlines of the sleeves. Don't overdo it, just strive for a coordinated effect that looks like custom designing instead of making do.

If a garment does not lend itself to rickrack application, there is another way to hide a let-down hemline. First, take out the old hem. Then carefully cut it off the dress at the faded hem mark. Insert the needed width of contrasting trim and sew the cut-off strip back onto the dress at the bottom of the attached trim. Repeat the design on a pocket or the edge of a sleeve. If your budget is really tight, you can use this trick without buying insertion trim. Just cut a length of solid color fabric that matches the garment and use that for the insertion. It is even possible to plan ahead for such tactics. At one time I made Karen a navy blue dress with tiny red and white flowers. Since the color was somewhat dark for a four year old, I relieved the severity of the print by putting on a white collar and white cuffs. A year later, when she needed extra length, a strip of white inserted at the hem added the perfect touch. Using a tiny decorative stitch around the collar, cuff, and insert, I pulled the whole thing together into a coordinated effect that didn't look "make do" at all.

Make It Do

One of the make-it-do things I remember most vividly from my childhood was the homemade grater my grandmother used when she made cream-style corn. I don't know why she didn't have a store-bought grater. Perhaps they weren't available in the small town where we lived or perhaps she didn't have the money to buy one, but, whatever the reason, my grandmother used what she had available and made it do. Her grater was an aluminum screw-on type lid through which my father had punched a series of nail holes. The result was a surface which looked a great deal like that on a regular grater, and it worked as well too.

Even though we may not have to be quite as thrifty as my grandmother was, it is still worthwhile to practice economy in all the ways we can. Frequently we are too quick to discard some household object that still has use in it—if we are willing to consider either repairs or alternate uses.

Bed sheets are one of my favorite make-it-do sources. Since sheets tend to wear out mostly in the middle, there frequently is useable fabric left on either side. When I was in my teens, my mother made me a pair of curtains from such a sheet. The curtains were made cafe style, and she trimmed them with two rows of bright yellow fabric strips. When those snowy white curtains were starched and hung at the window, no one would ever have guessed their origin was a discarded sheet.

Since most of us have a limited supply of old sheets, it is not a bad idea to learn to make do with new ones too. Look for orphan flat sheets at white sales. They can be turned into tablecloths, quilt linings, curtains, ironing board covers, and even articles of clothing. Since a sheet is so wide, it offers you more value per yard than does buying a similar amount of material from a bolt at the fabric store. A good quality percale sheet is finely woven and usually is permanent press. Consequently, it is just as good for making clothing as is material from the fabric store.

The kitchen offers numerous opportunities for learning to make do. You don't have the chocolate squares your brownie recipe requires? Substitute three tablespoons cocoa and one tablespoon cooking oil for each one-ounce square of unsweetened chocolate your recipe specifies, and the baking results will be identical. You have started to make a cake and discover that you have no cake flour? Don't drive to the store. Instead, use seven-eighths cup of all purpose flour for each cup of cake flour. You are ready to pour buttermilk into that special dish you always make for company dinners and you discover that all the buttermilk is gone? Simply add either a tablespoon of vinegar or lemon juice to a cup of whole milk to sour it and use it in place of the buttermilk you needed for your baking.

One of my favorite make-it-do recipes comes from a time when, in spite of our rather dismal financial situation, I was making a determined effort to stay at home as a full-time homemaker. We were eating a lot of beans and hamburger casseroles in those days, but I frequently found myself thinking of serving something really wonderful. What I had in mind was that old southern favorite, country-fried steak. But how could I do that on my limited budget? Well, I did it—sort of. Here is my "steak" recipe: Divide a pound of lean ground beef into eight equal portions. Cover a cookie sheet with aluminum foil and then flatten the ground beef into ultra-thin "steaks." (Each patty should be at least five inches in diameter.) Put these into the freezer. After they are frozen solid, you are ready to cook them. Crack a whole egg into a bowl and beat it. Heat cooking oil while you prepare the meat. Dip the thin, frozen "steaks" into the beaten egg and then into flour so that they are completely coated. Fry them in the hot fat until they are nicely browned on both sides. Remove them from the pan, drain the oil and return the meat to the pan. Add water, one or two bouillon cubes, the pan drippings, and more flour if you want a thicker gravy. Simmer for about a half hour until the gravy is thick and the aroma is magnificent. Serve the "steak" and gravy and don't tell everything you know!

It Takes a Family to Make a Home

Is Anybody Perfect?

Did you ever know a homemaker who seemed almost too good to be true? She cleaned and baked and refinished old furniture and did needlepoint and served as president of the PTA and even canvassed for the crippled children's fund. Just being in the room with this paragon was sufficient to give the average homemaker an aching case of the "my-achievements-will-never-match-hers" blues.

In spite of all the outward signs of domestic achievements, you may have noticed that something was wrong. Her family was not a happy one, and beyond the sparkling kitchen floors and the aroma of freshly baked breads were the sounds of bickering and discontentment. What could be wrong in the household of the "perfect" homemaker?

The problem obviously was not a lack of skill in the area of household achievements or even a failure to show concern for others. Perhaps, then, it was a matter of attitude and a failure to establish priorities as to what making a home actually consists of. "Homemaking" is a simple word. But unlike other simple words such as "dishwashing" or "skiing," which are also quite obvious, "homemaking" seems open to some strange interpretations.

Do you remember when you were a child and your mother said, "You must learn to keep house and to do the laundry because one day you will be a homemaker too"? Then in your high school home economics course you were probably told, "We are going to study budget planning, cooking, sewing, and many of the other things you will need to know to be a homemaker."

Somehow, the concept of homemaking seems to have become entangled with the practical matters of housekeeping. Such things as cooking, cleaning, and doing laundry are part of homemaking, but the real foundation of the meaning of the word is precisely what the word states: making a home. That is why the family who lives inside the house must come first. The family is more important than is cleaning or participating in civic affairs or adding creative touches designed to impress—or intimidate—other homemakers. Maintaining a smoothly running household is not the sum of homemaking. Rather, good organization and effective management are merely tools the homemaker uses to eliminate problems and to acquire time for the more vital elements of her career.

First Things First

But where do we start?

Deuteronomy 6:6-7 offers the answer: "And these words, which I command thee this day, shall be in thine heart: And thou shalt teach them diligently unto thy children, and shalt talk of them when thou sittest in thine house, and when thou walkest by the way, and when thou liest down, and when thou risest up."

The basis for Christian homemaking is not a Sunday morning religion but a dedicated commitment that goes on all the time—the kind of commitment that makes talking about spiritual things and living a Christian example a natural part of homemaking. No matter how hectic our schedule or how tiring our work, as Christian homemakers we must make time for the most important duty of all: helping to instill in our families faith that will sustain them for a lifetime.

One of the first steps in doing this is to establish a family devotional time. Reading the Bible and having prayers are not the only methods of teaching our children, because they do see our daily actions and learn from them, but while teaching Christian values to children is a constant process, the value of taking the family aside for daily devotions cannot be overlooked either.

Even if you have been a Christian for ten years or more, the first time you pray out loud during family prayer time you still may feel a bit awkward. The family knows you, and the first time you try praying for peace on earth, Junior is likely to inquire why you want the Russians and the Chinese to get along when you can't even get along with daddy.

Perhaps one of the reasons family altars are so hard for many families to start is that parents don't know how to get started. The best way is simply to get going with it. The bumps will smooth out as you go along, and you will learn to tailor family worship time to specific family needs. Meanwhile, you may want to look over some of the ideas which have worked for my family and decide if any of these are applicable to your situation:

Set a specific time.   For my family the best time for devotions is just before Karen's bedtime, but other families like mornings or the time right after the evening meal. It doesn't really matter which time of day you decide on; the important thing is to be consistent. Schedule devotion time into your day and stick with your appointment as faithfully as you would with any other engagement.

Keep it short.   There is no need to go on and on with devotion time. Children have short attention spans—and so do tired adults. I would rather know that one spiritual point was made and learned during our family's devotional time

124

than know a half dozen were spoken while minds wandered elsewhere.

Keep it informal. Avoid the temptation to pontificate. The family is not impressed with pompousness or pretended erudition. Just be yourself and give everyone else room to be himself too.

Be flexible. Although prayer and Bible reading are the main ingredients of the family altar, such things as songs, poems, and the telling of pertinent anecdotes that make a spiritual point can also be used. You might also want to use some printed devotional helps such as *Our Daily Bread.* If a three year old thinks singing "Jesus Loves Me" is the appropriate thing to do, then include that in the program as well. Spontaneity makes things interesting.

Let everybody participate. I can't imagine anything duller than being preached to by one family member every single night. Instead, we take turns leading the devotional time. The one who reads the Bible passage has the freedom to choose any Scripture he or she wishes and also to decide who will lead in prayer.

Be alert to special needs. Sometimes children bottle things up inside of them, and, with all the scurrying about adults have to do every day, it is difficult for them to slow their parents down long enough for a talk. Family altar time may be just the opening a child or even an adult needs to unload his concerns.

Don't be sidetracked. While you do want to be open to questions and discussions, it is necessary to guard against going off on inappropriate topics. Family altar time is not the place to answer, "Why can't I get a puppy?" Also, when devotionals are held at bedtime, older children are usually clever enough to realize that getting you started talking is a good way to put off going to bed.

Encourage independent study. The family altar is vital but it is not a substitute for private study. By the time a child learns to read, he can be encouraged to read his Bible privately too. Also, it helps to teach children to use such aids as maps, concordances, and Bible dictionaries. An answer they search out for themselves stays with them much longer than does the answer a parent glibly relates to them.

The Family Council

Being a homemaker means exposing yourself to one occupational hazard that none of us like: the possibility of turning into a nagging mother or wife. As executive vice-presidents in charge of housekeeping, it's easy for us to become irritated when the rest of the family either refrains from helping us or even creates additional work for us.

Who among us has not been guilty of beginning a sentence with "How many times do I have to tell you . . . ?" Sometimes it is hard not to feel sorry for yourself when you are running at full steam and everybody else in the family seems to be blithely coasting along on the fruits of your labors. For example: You try to keep a clean house, but nobody thinks twice about tracking mud into the kitchen. You declare war on clutter and disorder, but shoes and drinking glasses are still being left in the living room. You take a job to help boost the budget, but then you discover you get to keep all of your old chores in addition to all your new ones. That is enough to make a homemaker scream, or nag—or call a family council meeting.

If you are like me, you enjoy homemaking. It is a satisfying and fulfilling career. But the homemaking duties of themselves are not the problem. It is the reminding and the cajoling and—let's admit it—the nagging that get us down. No wonder we frequently ask ourselves if there might not be a better way.

There is a better way. For my family it was the formation of a family council. For years I had heard that this method of settling family problems could be effective, but it was not

126

until I reached the desperation point that I was willing to give the council idea a try. Here are some of the methods we used:

Set aside a regular day and hour.   We hold our meetings on Sunday evenings after church.

Set a time limit.   Grievances may go on and on if a specific time limit is not imposed. By having the meeting last only thirty minutes, all participants know they must have their facts ready and their reasoning straight before starting to speak.

Conduct the meeting in a spirit of helpfulness and an attitude of prayer.   Before we start, my husband prays and asks the Lord to guide us in our decisions. Then after the meeting is over we conduct our regular evening devotional.

Devise rules and impose them.   We have a strict rule that no one can bring up more than three grievances per meeting. This eliminates letting complaints go on and on. (Amazingly, after a few weeks of holding family council meetings, we discovered that most of us didn't have three grievances per week and some weeks we didn't have any!) Another rule, which Karen suggested, is that each complaint must be matched with a sincere compliment. It's hard to be grumpy about having a fault pointed out when you have just had a good quality admired at the same time!

Another firm rule is that no one can be interrupted during his specified turn. Even if no one else agrees with the speaker's opinions, the speaker is allowed to have his or her allotted time to have his say without interruption.

Keep records.   My family has recorded minutes of each family council meeting. The first order of business each week is to look back over the previous grievances and to praise those who have conscientiously worked to improve some weakness.

Have fun. The family council can solve many small problems which arise, but it is more than just a court of judgment. The idea is to bring the family together and to provide an uninterrupted period of time for the exchange of ideas about family concerns. It can also be the place for discussing such things as family vacation plans or it can be a forum for the expression of various opinions as to how a pay bonus should be spent or a time for discussing who should be invited to dinner next Saturday.

What are the advantages of a family council? Plenty! It gives each member of the family an equal opportunity to express personal views and to correct things that are bothering him. It also takes the pressure off during the remainder of the week. For instance, if Karen feels her bedtime should be a half hour later, she knows there is no need to ask about it every night of the week. Instead, she will be told to bring it up at the next council meeting. This gives her an opportunity to learn about strategy, preplanning, and negotiation. She knows that in order to sway our opinion she must come to the meeting solidly prepared. "Everybody else does it" is not an effective argument.

The family council is more than a means of determining family policy. It also provides an opportunity for sharing and for dispensing some needed back patting. In its simplest form, the family council can be defined as a means of keeping the family running smoothly by lubricating the small "pings" that could, if unattended, develop into major problems.

Not Enough Time with Daddy?

In spite of the differences in families, one of the most common factors is that children don't get as much time with their parents as they deserve. With more two-career mothers than ever before and with more fathers moonlighting an extra job and with more interest in sports and hobbies and with more pressure to keep up with current events and be an involved citizen, and, yes, with more emphasis on church activities, it

128

is a rare parent who spends as much time with his or her children as the children need. Certainly, we are frequently in the same place at the same time—everybody is sitting together on the same church pew or everybody is gathered around the television set or everybody is sitting in adjoining seats at the circus—but are we really *together?*

Togetherness as a family means much more than just being in the same building at the same time. It means sharing and listening and being conscious of each other's presence. But the problem is that these days all of us are busier than ever before. That is why we hear so much talk about the value of quality time over quantity time. But actually both are important. Sitting down for fifteen minutes to talk to a child is quality time but cuddling him in your lap while you watch television together or having him set the table while you peel the potatoes is the kind of quantity time that is still needed.

It is difficult at times for a two-career homemaker who comes home already tired, yet faced with cooking dinner and doing laundry, to feel enthusiastic about "help" in the kitchen, but children love to feel they are being included in adult chores. I might think that taking my daughter to the circus is a choice family activity, but she thinks baking brownies with me or washing the car with her father is just as exciting.

A recent survey by a respected pollster revealed that the average child gets two minutes of his father's undivided attention per day. That's appalling, isn't it? Of course, a father does have to make a living and he has to wash the car and mow the lawn and he may like to read newspapers or play golf, but still, he ought to find time for being a father too.

A mother automatically assumes that her two preschoolers will accompany her to the grocery store, the bank, and the beauty shop. Why shouldn't children also accompany their father on some of his rounds? Children need to learn about barber shops and sporting goods stores and car repair shops—but the best part is being with daddy.

Then there is the matter of quality time. I was impressed to learn how the principal of my daughter's school solves this problem. As the father of three girls, he came to realize that each one deserved some of his special, undivided attention, so he began taking one night of the week for an evening out with one of his young daughters. We liked this idea so well that we adopted it for our family too. Tuesday evenings belong to Randal and Karen. It begins with a meal together, usually at a spot we wouldn't choose if all of us were going—I'm not that fond of submarine sandwiches or banana splits! Then after the meal they might choose a game of miniature golf or some other activity they both like. Because of these "Daddy Days," Randal has begun to learn some of the things I've known all along—the kind of things children tell their mothers in that first talkative half hour when they come home from school: who the strictest teachers are, who sits across the aisle in history class, the joke the math teacher told, the poem for English class. It isn't always easy to make room for "Daddy Day," but the results are well worth the effort.

The Creative Homemaker

A Fulfilled Woman

Did you ever wonder what it would be like to have everything? Have you ever spent time daydreaming of what it would be like to have money, impressive clothing, and a husband who is constantly in the limelight?

A story has been recorded of a woman who fit this fantasy perfectly. Her husband was a well-known politician. She had a housekeeper and probably a cook as well. She could afford the most luxurious and expensive clothes available. No doubt, had she chosen to do so, she would have been able to live a life of complete leisure, never lifting a finger to sew up ripped clothing or to grow a garden or even to do comparison shopping at the market.

But this was not her choice. This woman was a diligent worker. Rising before the sun came up, she cooked breakfast for her family and for the household help. Then with this task—or privilege, as she probably saw it—behind her, she turned her thoughts and labors toward other work. She had clothing to sew, shopping to do, a garden to plant, and charity work to engage in. When all this was done, the woman devoted time to a home business that allowed her to bring in a little extra income while at the same time providing her with a relaxing outlet for her creativity.

Who was this extraordinary woman? The virtuous woman described in Proverbs 31:10-31. (This Scripture passage is probably not a description of an actual woman who once lived, but is a composite picture of all the desirable characteristics that a homemaker should have. The interesting thing about this passage is that the chapter opens with the information that this lesson was being taught to a king by his mother.)

One of the most significant things about this description of the ideal homemaker is that these verses contain so many references to her creativity. At first glance, it might seem incongruous that a woman, who was the wife of a politician (v. 23) and who had household help (v. 15) and who could afford the finest clothing (v. 22), spent so much of her time in creative pursuits. But out of a total of twenty-two verses, ten contain references to creative acts. It isn't only the creativity that is significant, however, it is the way in which the creativity was directed. With the exception of verse 22 ("She maketh herself coverings of tapestry; her clothing is silk and purple."), all the verses which describe this ideal homemaker's creativity either state or imply a creativity motivated by her concern for others. All that shopping, weaving, and gardening seems to have been, not just for the purpose of making this homemaker feel needed, but for the purpose of presenting a tangible and creative means of expression of her love for her family and for those in need.

Concern for others, then, is what being a creative homemaker is all about. We want to express our love for our families in the doing of little things and in the willingness to go the second mile. Baking a birthday cake for a child brings a mother a great deal of satisfaction, but is it the putting together of the ingredients of the cake that makes this such a joy or is it the anticipation of the happiness the cake will bring to the child? The anticipation of someone else's pleasure in a creative act should be our motivation.

Who Is a Creative Homemaker?

We have all met the kind of creative homemaker who makes the rest of us feel inadequate. She is the one whose kitchen floors shine like polished glass, even though she has just finished making twelve quarts of pickles—from cucumbers grown organically in her own garden, of course. Then, to make matters worse, she sits there serenely crocheting the most intricately patterned design you have ever seen while never missing a word of the conversation. There you are, feeling more and more inadequate by the minute as you gaze unappreciatively upon the masterpiece of a floral arrangement she has concocted out of dried natural materials. She serves you her own famous melt-in-the-mouth pound cake. "Oh, there's nothing to it," she protests as you ooh and aah. "Just take two dozen eggs and beat them precisely three minutes and six seconds at a room temperature of exactly 73.2 degrees. . . ." Quickly you finish your cake, pick up your belongings and your inferiority complex, and leave before you give in to that uncontrollable urge to ask if she also keeps a cow so that she can make her own homemade butter.

Fortunately for the self-esteem of the rest of us, there aren't too many homemakers like that. Otherwise, we might all become so demoralized that we would never again have the courage to exercise the necessary creativity to add fruit to gelatin.

Anything—including creativity—can be carried to extremes. Once we compare our creativity with that of other homemakers, we have already lost some of the joy in what we are doing. Creativity is an individual thing, and all of us do have a measure of it in some form. Maybe you can't make a souffle turn out right, but aren't you the one who gave all the preschoolers on the block such a good time by letting them help you cut out funny shapes from a roll of cookie dough? According to the dictionary, the word *creative* means "inventive," and, if that isn't inventive, nothing ever will be!

Being creative doesn't necessarily mean that you must be a whiz with knitting needles or that you must be a genius at thinking up ways to turn plastic margarine cups into works of art. Rather, being a creative homemaker means that you do the inventive kinds of things which bring happiness to you and your family.

Above and Beyond

Basically, then, being creative might be defined as doing that little something extra that makes your home a bit more pleasurable for you and your family. Forget about souffles and bobbin lace making and impressionistic painting if none of these things are right for you. Try what works best for *you*. Here are a few things that work for me:

Arrange some flowers. My idea of a perfect bouquet is one made up of wild daisies that my daughter Karen has picked for me. I "arrange" them by plopping the whole handful into an empty jelly jar. This amateurish effort will never win me any flower show prizes, but the bouquet brightens my kitchen and brings a favorable comment from each member of the family. An artistic arrangement of cattails and gold-sprayed Queen Anne's lace would be more elegant, but my wild daisies in their humble container represent "home" in a way no other bouquet could ever do.

Set a pretty table. Fortunately for my budget, I have never had a longing for expensive table settings, but I do like to make things look pretty. Thus, I have learned that mood and atmosphere do more for a dining room table than expensive crystal does. I prefer cloth napkins (made from a fabric remnant that cost me less than a package of paper napkins would have) for most family meals. Also I purchased a wide piece of red check tablecloth fabric for use when we picnic. That traditional red check pattern adds just the right festive touch, and I didn't have to pay tablecloth prices for it either.

Another thing we enjoy is noting holidays with appropriate table decorations. I buy paper decorations after the holiday and store them away for the next year's use. We also use candles on our dinner table occasionally.

Change your routine. What is it that makes us go on and on in the same routine year after year? Variety is still the spice of life. Change the furniture around. Try driving a different route to take the children to school. Serve soup, sandwiches, and fruit for breakfast and pancakes, bacon, and eggs for supper. Have a picnic breakfast in your back yard. Put a piece of work equipment, such as an ironing board or a sewing machine, in a different room. A new view can make the work more enjoyable.

Learn to enjoy the simple things. We live at such a hectic pace that we sometimes forget the pleasure to be had in sharing simple creative activities with our families. Being creative doesn't always mean *making* things. It can also mean *doing* things. Rediscover the joy of watching the sun come up and share it with a child. Put a bird feeder outside any window and learn to appreciate the beauty of the birds that come to visit. Take up star watching and, as a family project, learn the names of the constellations. Take time to enjoy the delicate, but cleverly-engineered beauty of a spider web glistening with morning dew—and if you don't have a child of your own, borrow one to share this wonder with. Give your appreciative husband a back rub. Who knows—he might even reciprocate!

Volunteer. The problem most of us have is too much commitment to outside activities, but if the host of meetings and commitments can be pared down to just one favorite volunteer activity, it is possible to regain the joy of expressing the creativity volunteering can bring. Choose one worthwhile commitment and then give it your very best.

Learn something new. Nothing fires the imagination as much as exposing it to new ideas. If you haven't thought of yourself as being a creative person, it isn't because you aren't—it's just because you haven't found the right outlet. Forget the idea that you must "find yourself" in only one creative outlet. Why not try a smorgasbord of activities? A lot of crafts I have tried were fascinating to do once, but I didn't want to start a life-long commitment. Why not enjoy painting one picture and then move on to enjoy knitting one sweater and then move on to learn silk flower making if that is your choice. When you hit the one thing that is most pleasurable for you, you will know it, and, in the meanwhile, you will have had the bonus of experiencing many creative outlets.

Try something you have never tried before. How do you know that you don't like Chinese food if you have never eaten it? Or how do you know that you can't make homemade bread if you have never tried? Or how can you be convinced that vacuuming is a woman's job and mowing the grass is a man's job unless you have tried switching the chores? How do you know that you can't paint a room or grow roses unless you give these things a try? Sometimes I think we have overrated the value of success. Who says you have to be the world's best in everything you do?

Work with children. If you think your creativity has gone dormant, a session as camp counselor or vacation Bible school teacher can wake you up to all sorts of possibilities. Want a challenge? Try looking at the cardboard core out of a roll of paper towels with a creative eye. Or, if you prefer, choose as your art medium such raw supplies as oatmeal boxes, potato chip cans, walnut shells, or macaroni products.

Don't overdo it. Why do so many of us feel that we have to keep proving ourselves? In particular, why is this so in the area of creativity? The idea of being creative is to enjoy doing things, not for the sake of impressing others, but for the pleasure to be found in using time unselfishly for doing something special for others. But don't overdo it. Something is dreadfully wrong when a homemaker can no longer buy anything ready made without chiding herself for it or when she cannot throw away potential craft materials, such as pine cones or egg cartons, without feeling guilty.

Give others the freedom to be creative too. As homemakers, most of us attempt to do too much, and the result is not only that we are frequently tired, but we also unwittingly deprive our family members of some of the pleasures they, too, might have had in exercising some creativity. It's easier to send a child outside to play so that you can bake a birthday cake without interference and it is easier to drive that child to the store to buy a birthday card for his father rather than to deal with the mess he will make with scissors and paste if he makes his own, but more than convenience is at stake here. It isn't enough to be a creative homemaker. You need to instill the joy of creativity in the rest of the family as well. One way of doing this is through the expression of appreciation for things that children make for you. For example, on one of my walls is an expertly crafted shadowbox made by a talented craftsman. It is unique and it draws many favorable comments, but sharing the honors on that same wall, is a plaque my daughter Karen made a few years ago in vacation Bible school. It is made of popsicle sticks painted brown and it has Bible verses glued on. It is an expression of my daughter's creativity and I like it!

Learn to take as well as give. Have you ever wondered why it is so much easier for most of us to do things for others than it is to allow others to do things for us? Yet one of the highest expressions of creativity is found, not in doing, but in allowing others the pleasure of doing for you. When I first married I didn't understand this and I used to protest when my mother would surprise me with a new dress she had made for me. I worried that she did such things because she thought we could not afford to buy new clothes. (We couldn't but we were doing our best to keep our poverty a secret from our parents!) As a consequence, I'm afraid I spoiled for her much of the joy she found in exercising her creativity. But now things have changed. My mother's eyes won't allow her to sew as she once did and I now surprise her with new dresses I have sewn for her. Much to her credit, she accepts them graciously and thus, lets me have the pleasure of enjoying my creativity to the fullest extent.

One of the things I have noticed about Jesus is that He allowed those who loved Him to express their love creatively when they chose to do so. Two incidents in particular stand out as examples of His acceptance of offerings of love. Mary, the sister of Martha and Lazarus, on one occasion anointed the feet of Jesus with an expensive ointment (John 12:1-8). While others criticized this action, Jesus accepted it and allowed Mary to express her love in this creative fashion. Later, when He was crucified, mention was made of a garment lovingly woven for Him by His mother (John 19:23-24). Jesus did not accumulate earthly possessions, but the one belonging that we do know about was one made for Him as a result of a mother's creative love.

My House Is Your House

The Practice of Hospitality

When I left home to attend college, I had a roommate who came from a large family. As two young women living away from home for the first time, both of us were a bit homesick, so it was inevitable that conversation frequently revolved around the topics of home and family. She told me about many of the exploits she and her brothers and sisters had enjoyed, and I, of course, told her that I had no brothers or sisters.

"What a lonely childhood you must have had," she replied sadly.

Lonely?

Such a thought had never occurred to me. As a matter of fact, I can scarcely remember a meal set with only enough plates for just my parents and me. It seemed somebody extra was always there. Several times one or both grandmothers were living with us. Widowed aunts, uncles who were out of work, and teen-age cousins all called our house home at one time or another. And, of course, plenty of out-of-town relatives came on weekends. I grew up thinking that wall-to-wall cousins sleeping on quilts on the floor was routine.

But my parents didn't only confine their hospitality to relatives. Everybody was welcome. There was a preschool boy from down the street who, for nearly five years, arrived pajama-clad in time for breakfast each morning. Later, a three-year-old girl next door started having her evening meal with us each day, and nobody seemed to think that was unusual either. But these were just the "regulars." We also had a frequent assortment of evangelists, pastors, and missionaries who were "just passing through" and needed a bed and a meal. Of course, these were made welcome too.

If an only child is supposed to be lonely, somebody forgot to tell my parents. Guests have always been just an ordinary part of their lives. For them, hospitality has never been a special kind of manners suitable for only auspicious occasions. Rather, the practicing of hospitality comes as naturally to them as does sneezing. In fact, I'd say if anyone has a gift for being hospitable, my parents do.

It has frequently been discussed whether hospitality is to be considered one of the gifts of the Spirit. The Bible lists eighteen definite, named gifts, but many feel that hospitality may also be included in this list. In his book, *Nineteen Gifts of the Spirit*, Leslie B. Flynn presents a convincing case for the inclusion of hospitality in the list of gifts. He explains that part of his reason for believing this is that in I Peter 4:9 we are commanded, "Use hospitality one to another without grudging." Then, in the next verse, Peter goes on to talk about the use of spiritual gifts. Flynn reinforces his position with Romans 12:13, in which Paul admonishes believers to be "given to hospitality."

Throughout the Bible, believers are urged to practice hospitality. Again and again, references are made to individuals who were outstanding in this respect. For instance, Paul was a tentmaker who lived for a time in the household of Priscilla and Aquila. In fact, Paul frequently depended on various Christian families to supply a temporary roof over his head as

140

he went about on his missionary travels. If hospitality had not been a dependable Christian trait, Paul, no doubt, would not have been able to do such extensive missionary work.

But what is hospitality? Most of us probably think of it in connection with inviting friends to Friday night dinner or to a Saturday afternoon cook-out. In other words, hospitality as we usually define it, means providing good food, good conversation, and good manners to those whom we have chosen to have in our homes. But the biblical meaning of hospitality goes much deeper. It includes those who are not quite so elite. In fact, Hebrews 13:2 even goes so far as to remind us to "Be not forgetful to entertain strangers. . . ."

This, then, is the ultimate test of Christian hospitality. Do you have room to lodge a missionary who has come to speak at your church? Is there space in your home for the unwed mother for whom your pastor is trying to find lodging? Do you have time on a hot summer day to offer a glass of water to the meter reader?

Matthew 25:35 contains a listing of some of the deeds which those on the right hand of Christ have done as evidence of their love for Him. Significantly, hospitality has a prominent place in this list: "For I was hungered, and ye gave me meat: I was thirsty, and ye gave me drink: I was a stranger, and ye took me in."

Even more significant is the answer of the King to those who question Him as to when they rendered these services to Him: "And the King shall answer and say unto them, Verily I say unto you, Inasmuch as ye have done it unto one of the least of these my brethren, ye have done it unto me" (Matt. 25:40).

Company's Comin'!

Years ago, there was a popular song that contained the oft-repeated phrase, "Company's comin'!" The music had a bouncy beat, and it was almost impossible to hear the tune without picking up on that joyful phrase and singing along with it. The person who wrote that song obviously liked having company and his feelings about the matter rang out in his music.

Like that songwriter, most of us do enjoy knowing that company is coming. But many of us prefer to have company on our own terms. Some of the greatest blessings, however, come from finding joy in the unexpected.

I can remember only one time that I heard my mother express dismay that company was coming up the front steps. No matter how inconvenient an unexpected visit might be, she and my father have the knack of not only making the guest feel they were glad to have him in their home, but at the same time of making themselves genuinely glad too.

The one exception to their gladness came shortly after Randal and I became engaged to be married. Following a flurry of housecleaning, baking, and general sprucing up of both people and house, we were anticipating the arrival of Randal's parents for that all-important first social get together of the entire group of future in-laws. Suddenly, things weren't going according to plans. Two minutes before the scheduled visit, a former neighbor—whom we had barely known—arrived at the front door unannounced. Suffice it to say that this woman, who had her approximately three hundred pounds rather snugly clad in shorts, had a loud voice, definite opinions, and the unsettling habit of casually including rather colorful expressions into her shouted-out conversation.

My parents conversed with this woman as politely as they did with Randal's parents and served her refreshments with just as much solicitude. In no way did they indicate that one guest was preferred over the other. I'm sure Mrs. Mouth felt just as well received as did my future in-laws. When the ordeal was finally over, my mother burst into giggles.

"Well, maybe it was all for the best after all," she concluded philosophically. "After today, nothing any of us ever do should come as a surprise to your in-laws!"

Impossible as that day was, it taught me a lesson I have never forgotten. It was a lesson not in word but in deed. Hospitality is much more than just polite entertaining. It is also the ability to convey warmth and caring even to those who may not be precisely what you had in mind as guests.

Be Prepared!

The Boy Scouts have a motto which would be a handy one for homemakers to adopt too, particularly in the area of exercising hospitality. The motto is, "Be prepared," and it captures succinctly the essence of the difference between being able to relax in the presence of unexpected guests or allowing yourself to become a nervous wreck. The key is to have a pantry that is well prepared. After guests arrive is too late to worry about the dust on the living room furniture or the dishes in the sink. It is time to make the best of the situation and move on to what really counts: What are you going to feed them?

To cope with such a crisis, an emergency guest menu can be a lifesaver. Anybody who wanders in unannounced has no right to be offended even if you serve him peanut butter sandwiches, but it is nice to have some preplanned reserves ready.

The first item in my disaster plan is a collection of quick-to-cook specialties. What is needed are some easy-to-handle recipes for some basic dishes with ingredients so common that you are bound to have them on hand and preparation steps so uncomplicated that you would have a hard time messing them up. A fluffy omelet is one dish that comes to mind immediately. It is appropriate for breakfast, lunch, or dinner, and even if the pantry is nearly bare, you will probably at least have a few eggs on hand. Another quickie for me is a one-pan coffee cake with a cinnamon, brown sugar, and butter topping. It is mixed in the baking pan and takes about forty minutes to prepare, which includes thirty minutes baking time. (Use any simple one-layer cake recipe you like or even keep one of those boxes of one-layer cake mix on hand if you prefer. Then top the uncooked batter with a mixture of one-third cup of brown sugar and a half-teaspoon of cinnamon. Cut two tablespoons of margarine into tiny pieces and dot the topping with margarine. Bake in a square cake pan at 350° and serve it warm.)

My other specialty is hot, homemade biscuits. For some reason, guests seem especially appreciative of these. A pan of biscuits seems to detract from any other shortcomings a hastily contrived meal might have.

Also I like to keep some just-in-case canned goods ready in the pantry. Two old standbys are pears and canned luncheon meat. Admittedly, this luncheon meat is not gourmet fare, but when a thin slice is nicely browned and served with a cheese slice in a split homemade biscuit, it does nicely. The canned pears are for a salad. I like to keep fresh salad makings on hand all the time, but just in case I don't have them, a pear half topped with a dollop of mayonnaise, some bits of shredded cheese, and a red cherry makes a colorful substitute. In these days of convenient frozen vegetables, most of us will have on hand some sort of vegetable for a rounding out of that meal for unexpected company. (If you don't have enough of one kind of vegetable, try combining such things as beans with peas or corn with lima beans, or canned tomatoes with frozen okra slices, or green beans with small chunks of potatoes.)

If you have a freezer, there is nothing better for coping with unexpected guests than pulling out a container of your own homemade soup. Just start that marvelous concoction bubbling and, once that aroma begins wafting out of the kitchen and into the living room, you will be well on your way to being voted the best cook in town.

Not all unexpected guests stay for dinner, but, even if they don't, you will probably want to offer them some sort of refreshment during the visit. Depending on the season, I keep on hand ingredients for hot cocoa or cold lemonade. Neither of these is costly or time consuming to prepare, but they do seem to imply that you think your guests are special enough to warrant a measure of pampering.

Regardless of what you choose for your "just in case," there is one thing that is even more important than the choos-

144

ing of the menu. Whatever you serve, make sure there is an abundance of it. Always serve your guests more than you think they will eat. This feeling of plenty creates a gracious effect that even candlelight and lace tablecloths could never achieve. Even if your menu consists only of ordinary foods such as omelets and biscuits, the fact that these things are in abundance implies to your guests that having them there is not an imposition and it leaves them the freedom to eat without first counting the biscuits.

Even more important than food preparation is a good attitude on the part of the hostess. In feeding unexpected guests, I strive to remember that the fellowship is just as important as the food and, with that thought in mind, I can serve bologna sandwiches and canned soup if the need arises.

This is something I learned—the hard way, of course—when I had not been married very long. Our pastor and his family unexpectedly came by our house one Sunday evening after service. Because I had not anticipated the visit, I had made no meal preparations. First, I tried to ignore the problem. If I didn't say anything, they would assume we had already eaten. But the pastor had young children, and I began to realize they had not eaten either. Finally I swallowed my pride and invited the pastor's wife to accompany me to the kitchen. There we opened cans of soup and tuna fish, took bologna and cheese out of the refrigerator, and set the peanut butter jar on the table. Not knowing what anyone liked, I decided to let everyone concoct his own sandwich. Then, discovering I had no canned fruit or anything else sweet, I spied a box of marshmallow cakes. Those were our dessert.

The result? That night was the beginning of a special friendship with the pastor's family. In fact, that occasion turned out to be one of the most successful "dinner parties" I've ever had.

Getting Ready for Company

How do you prepare for guests? Do you scurry about cleaning this and polishing that and straightening closets and vacuuming corners? I used to do that too. Then one day an amazing thought occurred to me: most of the special things I do before company comes I would have to do again after my company leaves. This doesn't mean that I gave up on house-cleaning. Instead, I try to accept the fact that what is good enough for my family on an everyday basis is certainly good enough for guests on a short-term basis.

Then there is the matter of the smallest guests. It makes sense to me to put away valuable breakable objects before they arrive. I wanted my daughter to learn to live with such things, so I never put anything away when she was small. I have discovered, however, that some of my friends have dif-fering views on raising children and while I preferred teach-ing Karen to leave decorative objects alone, other parents prefer to simply have the possible temptation removed. Thus, if I feel it makes young guests and their parents more comfortable to have such things out of the way prior to the visit, I just collect them and store them out of sight. Hos-pitality hinges on the preference of the guests and not on the preference of the hostess.

Another thing I have learned about hospitality comes from my aunt. She entertains guests by letting them be part of the family. Because she accepts everyone as "family" in-stead of company, she has little preparation to do before guests arrive. For instance, if she is going to have fresh peas for dinner, she will invite guests to go with her to the garden to pick them and then afterward she will place comfortable chairs out on the porch for everybody to use while shelling the peas. As a result of my aunt's attitude, everybody likes to visit her.

The best idea for preparing for hospitality is to let the rest of the family in on the fun. Think back to your own child-hood. Can't you almost feel once again that racing sense of excitement you knew when somebody special was coming to visit? If so, you can also remember that the thing that made the visit especially wonderful was that you were allowed in on the preparations. That is why it is so important that your children be allowed to help too. A wonderful event that is about to take place gains even more excitement when it becomes an occasion for participation by the entire family. You may be startled to discover that the child who couldn't stand to polish furniture last week as a routine chore doesn't mind half as much when he is made to feel that he is making an important contribution to increasing Grandma's pleasure in her upcoming visit.

The Hostess with the Mostest

If someone were to poll you on the household you visited where you felt the most enjoyment, what would you remember? Would you think of elegant souffles and finely decorated rooms or would you bring to mind times of fun and relaxation?

Most likely, the memories you have of the places where you had the best visits don't have much at all to do with such things as furniture or elegance of dining. Rather, most of us like to go where we are made to feel wanted and special.

That is why the hostess who is most highly thought of does not have to be the one with the most expensive china or the most elaborate home decor. Rather, she is the one who cares about each guest and puts his needs first. She doesn't force conversation on those who don't feel like talking. She doesn't plan outings as a "surprise." She doesn't force guests who don't like games to play them.

Her concern is not for what she thinks makes for a lovely evening but for what her guests like best. Through this serving of the needs of others she finds herself reflecting the values taught by the Savior.

And Then There Was One . . .

Is One a Family?

Some months ago I was invited to speak to a women's group of a local church. As is my custom, before preparing my talk I asked the program coordinator to tell me a few important facts about the individuals in the group. Were most of them married women or single women? What was the age range? Were most of them mothers? Her answers revealed that the group was one with mixed interests—something of a problem for a speaker who was to talk for thirty minutes on homemaking. It is fairly easy to discuss homemaking with young married women who still have children in their homes, but what common homemaking interests do single women, elderly women, widows, empty-nest mothers, and mothers of preschoolers all have in common?

As I began to think about the audience and I began to pray and to study my topic, I came to a realization: homemaking is not reserved exclusively for the traditional stay-at-home mother with the ideal family consisting of a hardworking

148

husband and the average two children. Instead, homemaking, in its truest sense is something which even single women and empty-nest mothers do. Homemaking means "making a home," and, even if you are the only person in that home, you need some care and pampering too.

Home is a place where we are safe from the attacks of the outside world. Within its comforting walls no work pressures or overbearing bosses or irritable customers or impatient co-workers can reach us. While we may have to go out the next morning and face the same problems again, the brief respite provided by the home gives us the recharge necessary to enable us to face the world once more.

That is why home is so important to all of us, but especially so for the single woman. While some homemakers have understanding husbands to listen to their troubles and to give the needed support for coping with problems, the single woman has no such convenient shoulder to cry on. Thus, for her, it becomes even more important to develop a sense of home that can give her the kind of sheltered feeling she needs. Making a home is not only to be done for a husband and children, it is also something a woman does for her own well being.

In today's society, most women will, at one time or another, find themselves living alone. Many women are choosing not to marry at all, and, of those who do, many are marrying later than previous generations of women. Then there is the factor of divorce. With current statistics showing one divorce for nearly every two marriages, more and more women are finding themselves unexpectedly single for the second time. Add to this the fact that statistics show a longer life span for women than for men, and it all comes out to an increased likelihood that most homemakers will, sooner or later, experience some time of living alone.

Who Is My Family?

For the single woman, the absence of husband and children means the absence of a great many obligations. Consequently, the single woman has an even greater opportunity to share her homemaking with others than the wife and mother could ever have. The single woman has a career and housework and laundry to do, but the volume of work required in her household is considerably less.

The Bible recognizes the spiritual contributions which single women are able to make as a result of their unmarried state. I Corinthians 7:34 describes the difference in mental attitude between married and unmarried women. Since the unmarried woman has no husband to answer to, she finds it easier to dedicate herself more fully to the Lord's service than does the married woman who may care more for pleasing her husband.

For the single woman, the word *family* takes on a new meaning. Because the single woman has no husband and no children at home, she may "adopt" others as part of her homemaking. In thinking of some of the single women I have known, those who seemed happiest were those who found creative outlets which offered them an opportunity to share their home with others.

An example of this kind of unmarried woman was Dorcas. Although the Bible does not specifically define Dorcas as a single woman, it appears that she may have been. No mention is made of a husband or children being present to mourn her death, although many widows were with her. Thus, it seems that Dorcas might have been a widow too. The significant thing about this woman was that she had stretched out her homemaking to include many of her friends and neighbors. In Acts 9:36 we are told ". . . this woman was full of good works and almsdeeds which she did." Verse 39 notes that Peter came to the place where Dorcas was and ". . . all the widows stood by him weeping, and shewing the coats and garments which Dorcas made, while she was with them." Here was a homemaker whose ministry to the "family" was such that even after her death friends were still talking of her good deeds.

The Empty-nest Homemaker

Is a homemaker still a homemaker when the children are gone? Most definitely! Just as the single woman with only herself to make a home for qualifies for the homemaker title, so does the woman whose children have grown up and made separate homes for themselves. In a manner similar to that of the unmarried woman, the empty-nest homemaker may even discover that there are certain advantages to her new lifestyle. Instead of meeting the many demands of a growing family, she now has more hours to call her own. As a consequence, she can find new and challenging outlets for her homemaking.

Yet many women find this stage in their lives quite depressing. As one woman explained it, "I'd spent all those years being Mama and then quite suddenly I had worked myself out of a job." After the initial shock of the empty nest, however, most Christian homemakers make an amazing discovery: they are still needed. Their range of service has changed, but grownup offspring do still need their mother. They just need her in a new capacity.

Just as the unmarried woman has the option of defining "family" outside of blood ties, so does the empty-nest homemaker. With our nation being one where job transfers are commonplace and young couples frequently live thousands of miles away from their parents, there is a desperate need for stand-in Christian "parents." In fact, this can be one of the most satisfying ministries a "retired" homemaker can undertake and it is even more satisfying when approached as a joint effort of both husband and wife. Somehow, the sharing of a special event such as Christmas with those who are unable to share it with their own families helps to bring back some of the glow most of us thought holidays had lost.

Older women may also have a gift for counseling. Having lived many years as a Christian homemaker, a woman certainly has the experience to counsel younger women. Titus 2:4-5 shows that the opportunity for teaching goes beyond that of family ties. The older women are given a charge "that they may teach the young women to be sober, to love their husbands, to love their children, To be discreet, chaste, keepers at home, good, obedient to their own husbands, that the word of God be not blasphemed." We would like to think that in raising our daughters we have instilled in them all the values they will need for successful homemaking, but this may not be true. In fact, younger homemakers are greatly in need of both the counsel and the example of older Christian women whom they can depend on. Whether the problem be the discipline of children or the making of an apple pie, it is a fortunate young homemaker who can be "adopted" by an older homemaker with the wisdom to advise her in a spiritual manner.

Empty-nest homemakers may also find pleasure in engaging in volunteer services for others. While younger homemakers are juggling schedules and trying to pare down outside activities, the empty-nest homemaker may find that, as far as volunteering is concerned, the time is right. A friend of mine learned that helping others is often the way to help yourself—particularly if loneliness is a problem. This woman found her lifestyle suddenly rearranged. Not only was her husband being transferred to a distant city where the couple would be far from married offspring and grandchildren, but, at the same time, their youngest child was leaving for college on the opposite side of the country. But what could have been a time of depression for this woman turned out to be a time of blessing. Almost immediately upon arrival in the new city, she volunteered to work one day a week at the hospital. There she willingly spent time with others who had no families to visit them, and, in helping others, she found she had also helped herself.

Another opportunity for the sharing of home is found in the "adopting" of missionary families. At our church, all of us have missionary families which we have "adopted" and, by contributing to their financial support, writing letters to them, and remembering their birthdays, we are able to do a little long-distance homemaking. Those of us with families, jobs, and children, however, don't seem to have quite the skill at this that some of the older women have. They may have more time to write letters and they have the depth of Christian experience which makes them good "listening ears" for young missionary families who normally would not discuss their homesickness or frustrations with other Christians.

Homemaking, like Christianity, has no retirement age. Whether it be making a home for husband and children or spreading a bit of "home" to those who may not even be kinfolks, the Christian homemaker has a ministry that extends through an entire lifetime.

But What If I Fail?

The Enemies of Homemaking

"The hand that rocks the cradle rules the world" is a powerful statement still true today. Given the importance of the home and the importance of the influence a homemaker exerts within that home, it is inevitable that Satan will do his best to disrupt the home. It is not a matter of coincidence that the most distressing problems which individuals can encounter are also the ones which undermine the foundation of the family as well. Alcoholism, juvenile delinquency, adultery, money problems, gambling, drug addiction, and divorce are just a few of the problems which tear families apart.

Yet these serious problems are not the only ones causing disruption. Big problems usually have their roots in small happenings and sometimes in actions which don't seem at first to be of much consequence.

Proverbs 14:1 draws the dividing line between the actions

of the successful homemaker and the actions of the destructive homemaker: "Every wise woman buildeth her house: but the foolish plucketh it down with her hands."

The literal meaning of the Hebrew word which has been translated "plucketh" is "to break or to throw down." Thus, it seems that the foolish homemaker is, through her own deeds, responsible for the discarding of her values about her home. These are a few of the elements which can cause that breaking down:

"I" trouble. The philosophy of "do your own thing" has no place in the Christian home. In order for home to be a place of stability, each family member must think in terms of "we" and not "I."

Concern over what others think. A homemaker can make herself and her family miserable by constantly gauging her actions and her purchases in terms of the effect it will have on others.

Too much desire for material things. I once knew a bride who couldn't rest until she had everything. It seemed beyond her comprehension that most married couples accumulate a house full of furniture over a period of years. She had to have hers immediately. Then, of course, that fine furniture necessitated the purchase of a new house. This, in turn, meant the purchase of a new car for the driveway. Nothing seemed to satisfy this woman. Each new purchase merely sparked her desire for more things. The problem was, she wasn't the wife of a millionaire, but rather the wife of a man with a typical middle-class income. Within a year this couple did have everything: furniture, house, car, installment debts, arguments, and divorce.

Feelings of inferiority. Sometimes it is difficult for homemakers to resist comparing their achievements with the achievements of others. But God made each of us as we are, and, while He may have given your sister-in-law or your neighbor certain talents which He didn't choose for you, He also gave you certain attributes that He didn't give to them.

Not enough togetherness.   One of the most disturbing factors about family life today is that everybody is rarely at home at the same time. Conflicting schedules seem to turn the front door of the house into a revolving door.

Too many good causes.   For the Christian, it is especially important to take part in worthwhile activities in addition to church activities. We would like to think that, as well as being active church members, we are also concerned citizens and caring humans. That is why we frequently find ourselves, in addition to carrying a full load at church, participating in consumer causes, environmental causes, humanitarian causes, and school causes. The problem arises when too many good causes are taken on simultaneously. The family is still the most important "good cause" a homemaker can support, and, unless the family comes before volunteer activities, the home is in trouble.

The wrong kind of entertainment.   Jokes are made about homemakers being hooked on soap operas. Yet it hardly seems a joking matter. These programs tear down the very values which homemakers want for their families. Not only is time spent with the soaps a waste of a valuable portion of the homemaker's day, but there is another more dangerous aspect to the problem. Have you ever noticed how those who are especially fond of this type of programming start to imitate soap opera plots? Somehow an involvement with this sort of television fare seems automatically to cause a viewer to develop a suspicious and scheming outlook on life.

Another common factor with soap opera addicts is that they start to think of the story characters as real people. Thus, day after day, the viewers are influenced by seeing their "friends"—who, after all, are "nice" people—doing such things as enjoying cocktails, dressing immodestly, and having affairs. As a result, it becomes easier and easier to think that perhaps those things aren't so sinful after all.

156

It has been said that "you are what you read" and when it comes to homemaking this is especially true. What we take *into* our minds exerts a tremendous influence on what comes *out* of our minds. It is important that Christian homemakers learn to choose their reading material wisely. "Racy" novels such as those currently being printed under the euphemistic label of "historical romances" can in no way add to Christian values.

"But Did You Read the Instructions?"

I am hopeless when it comes to putting together swing sets or bookcases or bicycles. Even looking at the diagrams doesn't help. That line drawing of "bolt A" and "slot B" looks identical to "bolt R" and "slot Q" to me. Nevertheless, there have been times when I have been impatient to get some article assembled and, instead of waiting for my husband to handle the task competently, I plunged right into it. The result? Once I assembled a stand for a portable television set and had half a dozen parts left over. Not only that, the surface that was supposed to be flat tilted at an odd angle, the front wheels wouldn't turn at all, and the back wheels kept rolling off.

"How did you do *that?*" Randal asked in disbelief when he saw the results of my work. "Did you read the instructions?"

"Well, I was in a hurry," I excused myself.

"But did you read the instructions?" he asked again.

"I didn't think I'd understand them if I read them," I defended myself. "You know those diagrams all look alike to me."

"If all else fails, try reading the instructions," Randal said as he reached for the screwdriver and began undoing my entire afternoon's work.

Later, as I thought about that episode, I saw something in it besides my inability to assemble a television stand. I recognized in myself a human characteristic that gets a lot of people—including me—into trouble.

It is easy to plunge into the task at hand. It is not so easy to take time to think about a task and to plan for it and to ask God's blessing on it before we start. Yet plunging in is the way we want to do things most of the time. "It takes too long to read the instructions," I might have said. But how much time did I waste in going about my job in the wrong manner? And just what good did all that effort accomplish? It was sincere but it didn't work.

The same thing is true of many of our homemaking duties. "It takes too long to read the instructions," we complain as we skim a Bible passage instead of studying it carefully. "I probably couldn't understand it even if I did read it," we add in an attempt to justify our actions.

Yet the Bible—God's set of instructions for the job to be done—is waiting to help us avoid putting our lives together in a tilted, ramshackle manner. Unlike that ill-assembled television stand, our lives cannot be taken apart later and put back together again so that no one will ever know the difference. God can take away the sin and can bring order into our lives when we ask Him to do so, but the scars of those years spent in ignoring His instructions will always be left as a reminder that it pays to read the instructions first.

Any homemaker can find satisfaction in her homemaking career by doing it "unto the Lord" and by daily seeking His guidance. The same heavenly Father who knows when a sparrow falls also knows—and cares—when a homemaker is weary or perplexed or discouraged. Therefore, learning to go to Him daily for our set of instructions is essential: "Hearken unto the voice of my cry, my King, and my God: for unto thee will I pray. My voice shalt thou hear in the morning, O Lord; in the morning will I direct my prayer unto thee, and will look up" (Ps. 5:2-3).

158

Roundup of Ideas

Roundup of Ideas

- An old-fashioned dessert offers an opportunity to use up slightly stale bread. Here is my mother's recipe for bread pudding: Preheat oven to 350°. Crumble four slices of bread into a bowl. Pour one and one-half cups of milk over the bread and let this stand for fifteen minutes. Meanwhile, melt one-fourth cup of butter or margarine and add it to the bread and milk mixture. Add two eggs, one teaspoon of vanilla, and three-fourths cup of sugar to the mixture and mix well. Bake in an eight-inch pan for about fifty minutes or until a toothpick inserted in the center comes out clean. For a fancier dessert add nuts, coconut, raisins, or fruit such as drained pineapple.
- Onions won't make you cry when you peel them if you keep them under water and keep your mouth closed while peeling them.
- Store leftover bits of lace, binding, and rickrack by

wrapping them around the core from a roll of paper towels. Secure the ends by putting a pin or tack through the lace and into the hollow core.

- To make a firmer meatloaf with a different taste use uncooked oatmeal instead of bread crumbs and substitute tomato cocktail juice for the tomato sauce you normally use.

- Spreading pizza dough in a pan is easy if you dip your fingers in warm water and keep the dough slightly damp as you spread it.

- For a quick, no-cost bulletin board, ask the fabric store for an empty styrofoam fabric bolt. By wrapping a length of fabric around it and attaching a hanger, you can have a free bulletin board that matchès your curtains or bedspread or whatever you choose.

- To avoid the mess involved in slicing cake for a child's birthday party, bake cupcakes instead and place them in rows. Then put one letter on each cake so that when lined up the cupcakes spell out "Happy Birthday." The birthday child and the children who win the games you play receive the cupcakes with the candles on them.

- It is more economical to operate a refrigerator when the coils are kept clean, but it is difficult to get a cleaning tool into the coil area. Fasten a bottle cleaning brush to a wooden ruler or to a short length of broomstick and you have a coil cleaner that is both effective and convenient to use.

- To store sweet onions so that they will not rot, use an old pair of hosiery. Put one onion in the toe, tie a knot, put in another onion, and so on. Hang this in a cool, dry area. The onions will keep much longer than they do in a storage bin.

- If you are installing inlaid linoleum in your kitchen, don't discard the large piece that must be cut out to go around your kitchen cabinets. It is the right shape and size to fit the cabinet floor under your sink.

- Do you need a large scoop for such things as dipping out dry pet food or grass seed or lawn food? If so, use a clean gallon-size plastic container (such as the kind used for bleach, fabric softener, or milk) and, beginning just below the handle, cut downward to remove the side and the entire bottom. Leave the opposite side intact and you will have a large scoop, complete with handle, that is just right for many purposes. (Be sure to check the screw-on lid occasionally to make sure it is tightly secured.)

• One of the handiest "tools" a woman driver can carry in her car is a plastic squirt bottle such as the kind dishwashing detergent comes in. Fill it with clean water, and it can be used to add water to the car battery or to the radiator. It can also be used as an emergency source of water when a child spills something on the upholstery or for washing dirty hands.

• Spray cans of fabric protector and water repellent are good for much more than just revitalizing your raincoat. They can also serve as a dirt barrier on framed fabric pictures, sofa pillows, dining room chair seats, and especially canvas purses.

• Keeping lint out of the bobbin area in your sewing machine will help keep your sewing trouble-free, but sometimes it is difficult to sweep all the lint out using a brush made for that purpose. For better results, buy the cheapest artist's brush you can find (look in the children's toy department beside the watercolor sets and coloring books) and use it to reach into those hard-to-clean areas.

• Did you get too much salt in the gravy or the corn? Peel a good sized potato, cut it into four chunks, and cook it briefly in the pan with the oversalted food. The potato will not impart enough of its own flavor to be noticeable but it will absorb some of the excess salt and enable you to salvage the dish you thought you had ruined. Before serving, remove the potato.

• If you have a blanket that is in good shape even though its color is faded and its binding is worn out, use it for the "batting" inside a quilt. Just insert the blanket between the patchwork top and the lining and, instead of quilting it in the traditional manner, tack it at intervals with colorful thread or yarn. (Tacking does not have to be done as closely spaced as quilting is done.) If you don't like piecing together fabric for quilt tops, buy a sale-priced length of quilt print fabric (five yards for a double bed). Insert the blanket between that and the lining and tack it. You will have a "quilt" in a very short time.

• Save your old magazines and buy an inexpensive photo

161

album (the kind with the lift-up plastic pages) as part of your "hospitality kit" when children come to visit. Provide the youngster with some blunt scissors and ask him to make up a scrapbook of cars or different kinds of vegetables or whatever else is pictured prominently in your magazines. Since no glue is involved, there is no mess. If you stock up on these albums when they are on sale, they will make nice take-home gifts for young visitors.

• Do you use clothespins? If so, storing them can be a problem. Here is an attractive clothespin bag which even a nonsewer can make: Use a little girl's dress in either a six-month or twelve-month size (these are cheap at garage sales). Turn it inside out and stitch across the ends of the sleeves and then sew the front of the dress to the back of the dress near the hem. Turn it right side out and hang it on a clothes hanger and it is ready for storing your pins. If you don't need a clothespin bag, this idea can also be utilized for making a storage bag for hosiery or, if you have a young daughter, a favorite outgrown dress can be further enjoyed as a sock container.

• A brick placed in the toilet tank displaces part of the water in the tank, thus saving quite a bit of water on each flush.

• If you need to peel a large quantity of tomatoes or peaches, use this quick method. Bring water to a boil in a large container. Put in five or six tomatoes or peaches and, after a few seconds, turn them over with a large wooden spoon. Dip them out with a tea strainer. Then put them into a bowl of cold water. The change in temperature will cause the skins to slip off easily.

• Most homemakers know that a box of baking soda in the refrigerator will absorb odors, but for even better results, start with a clean refrigerator that has been washed in water that has baking soda dissolved in it.

• When my daughter was small I found a special way to help her enjoy holidays. Using coloring books with large, simple designs, trace an applique pattern of a holiday motif such as a holly wreath or a Valentine heart. Cut pieces out of appropriately colored fabric and use the satin stitch on your

162

sewing machine to sew these together. Use a satin stitch to add features. Then, using a wide zig-zag stitch, apply these holiday motifs around the border of a skirt or, if you are short of time, center one large motif on the back of a vest. Using this wide zig-zag stitch will secure the design well enough to hold it on the fabric for a few wearings but will not make it so permanent that it cannot be easily removed when the holiday is over.

• Don't throw away your old plastic shower curtain. It makes a good drop cloth when you are painting or it can be carried in the trunk of the car for use as a ground cloth when such things as tire changing must be done.

• For children who are going away to camp, you can make an inexpensive alternative to toiletry cases. Cut a length off the leg of an old pair of jeans, making a tube about twelve to fifteen inches long. Sew across the bottom and then make a casing at the top and insert a drawstring. The result is a durable toiletry bag which can be washed and rewashed. If desired, personalize the bags with liquid embroidery paints.